Doctrine and Ethos in the Labour Party

For Nancy

Doctrine and Ethos in the Labour Party

H. M. DRUCKER
Senior Lecturer in Politics, University of Edinburgh

London
GEORGE ALLEN & UNWIN
Boston   Sydney

First published in 1979

GEORGE ALLEN & UNWIN LTD
40 Museum Street, London WC1A 1LU

© George Allen & Unwin (Publishers) Ltd, 1979

British Library Cataloguing in Publication Data

Drucker, Henry Matthew
    Doctrine and ethos in the Labour Party
    1. Labour Party
    I. Title

329.9'41   JN1129.L32   78–40899

ISBN 0–04–329026–4
ISBN 0–04–329027–2

Typeset in 10 on 11 point Plantin by Trade Linotype Limited, Birmingham
and printed in Great Britain
by Billing and Sons Limited, Guildford, London and Worcester

Preface

The Labour Party, and most of those who have written about it, take its intellectual pretensions too seriously. The purpose of this book is to argue that there is more to the party's ideology than socialist doctrines. Its ideology has been equally strongly influenced by the sentiments and traditions of the people who have created and controlled it. My argument is that the party is not simply an instrument for acquiring and using power – not simply a vote-gathering machine designed for policy making and implementation. The party has a life of its own – a fact which political scientists have acknowledged without taking sufficiently seriously. Even now, when so many of its early socialist doctrines have been discredited, and so much of its early working class ethos has been tempered by experience of government and diluted by middle-class recruitment, the party's ideology embodies both doctrine and ethos.

This book is not a history either of the Labour Party or of its ideology. Rather, it is an attempt to sort out the categories in which Labour's ideology can be understood. Because it is not a history, I have not sought to discuss issues in the order in which they have arisen in the course of the party's life. On the other hand, I hope that I have placed the individual actions and policies which I have discussed in their proper historical context. I have tried to make the ideas of the book as accessible as possible by writing simply and eschewing jargon. For the same reason, and particularly to make the book comprehensible to readers who may not be familiar with the party's history, I have appended a short chronology of important events.

I began to think about the Labour Party, and to try to comprehend it, almost as soon as I joined it in 1967. Two things struck me immediately: theoretical works about the concept of ideology were of little help in understanding the party's ideology; so – more surprisingly – were the works about British political parties. The party was marching to tunes which none of the writings had yet scored. As a member of the party I had heard tunes which I could not, as an academic, transcribe. Gradually, I began to puzzle out why this should be so. This book is the result.

I am grateful to my colleagues who have discussed some of the ideas in this book with me at seminars and conferences. I read a version of Chapter 1 at the Political Studies Association Conference in the spring of 1974: Chapter 2 is developed from a paper I read at the International Political Science Association Congress in the summer of 1976: I read an early version of Chapter 4 at a weekend school of the London School of Economics late in 1975. I am also grateful for comments on substantial parts of this book to Paul Addison, Rodney Barker, Gordon Brown, Michael Clarke, James Cornford, Bernard Crick, Stanislaw Erlich, Roy Gregory, Richard Gunn, Harry Hanham, David Kettler, George Lavau, Tom Nairn, Gary Soroka, David Welsh, Jerzy Wiatr and Paul Wilkinson. I alone am, of course, responsible for the book. I would also like to thank Kathy Brown, Joan Ludvik and Helen Ramm for typing the several drafts. But most of all I am indebted to my wife Nancy for her help at all stages of the writing. To her, with love, this book is dedicated.

H. M. DRUCKER

Edinburgh
March 1978

Contents

I
Two Dimensions of
Labour's Ideology

I

In April 1976, James Callaghan was selected as leader of the Labour Party, and hence Prime Minister, by a vote of his colleagues in the Parliamentary Labour Party. This was the first time that the Parliamentary Labour Party had chosen a man leader knowing he would become Prime Minister. Callaghan was only the fourth leader the party had chosen since its recovery in 1935 from the depths of betrayal and division in 1931. In that time, by contrast, there had been eight leaders of the Conservative Party. There had even been four monarchs (and one of them was forced out).

The Labour Party changes leader infrequently. Once it selects a man it is very reluctant to dispose of him against his will. Only Lansbury was forced out – in 1935. No Labour Prime Minister had been forced out. None has even had to defend his position in an election. And while the party has been in opposition the only leader to be challenged to an election was Gaitskell (by the importunate Harold Wilson, in 1960), and he was solidly supported even though his policies were unpopular in the party. That Wilson was not himself challenged in the years of Conservative government after his premiership of 1964–70 – when he was most unpopular – speaks worlds for the strength of Labour's tradition.

This traditional tenderness to its leaders is, I want to argue, an important part of Labour's ideology. In arguing in this way I am proposing to use the term 'ideology' in a rather broader way than is common amongst political scientists. I am proposing to use it to include the traditions, beliefs, characteristic procedures and feelings which help to animate the members of the party. This is not what commentators about the party normally have in mind when they talk of its ideology. Typically, they concentrate on the doctrinal aspects: they describe the party's behaviour as an institution as if it were a machine for the creation and propagation of socialist doctrine and the translation of that doctrine into policy, legislation and practice. Some commentators are impressed by the party's ability to translate its doctrines into practice; but the majority are not.

As against this exclusive emphasis on the doctrinal aspects of Labour's ideology I want to show first of all that the party's ideology contains another dimension, which I shall call its ethos, and then to emphasise the importance of this second dimension. Unwillingness to sack leaders is an expression of this ethos. Other expressions are: first, the way it hoards its money; secondly, the formality of its practices (i.e. their embodiment in written, often detailed, rules); and, thirdly, its demands for sacrifices from its leaders. Perhaps the best way to begin this discussion is with an analysis of the existing commentaries.

Recent writings about the ideology of the Labour Party admit of four main theses and one major modification. Chronologically, the first thesis was stated by R. T. McKenzie in *British Political Parties* (1963).[1] The second was stated by R. Miliband in *Parliamentary Socialism* (1961); it was substantially modified by Leo Panitch in 'Ideology and integration: the case of the British Labour Party', in *Political Studies* (1972).[2] The third is found in S. Beer, *Modern British Politics* (1965),[3] and the fourth in a series of papers by Tom Nairn, 'The nature of the Labour Party 1 and 2', and Perry Anderson, 'The origins of the present crisis', in the *New Left Review* (1964).[4] McKenzie, leaning heavily for theoretical support on Ostrogorski's *Democracy and the Organisation of Political Parties*, submits these gloomy reflections on the role of parties:

> The distribution of power within British political parties is primarily a function of cabinet government and the British parliamentary system. . . . But, whatever the role granted in theory to the extra-parliamentary wings of the parties, in practice final authority rests in both parties with the parliamentary party and its leadership. In this fundamental respect the distribution of power within the two major parties is the same.
>
> As was shown in Chapter 1 both major parties have consistently exaggerated the difference between their party organisations with a view to proving that their own is 'democratic' and that of their opponent is not.[5]

McKenzie's researches led him to minimise the role of ideology in both Conservative and Labour parties. All party activity is assumed to lead to – and hence to be fairly measured by – its ability to control parliamentary activity. The constant theme of this work is the ability or incompetence of the annual conference to control the Cabinet and the leadership. The answer McKenzie comes up with, of course, is that annual conference controls neither.

This lack of control is taken to show that the party is not democratic. Whether or not we accept Professor McKenzie's single-minded concern with the supposed democracy of the policy-making process, this is surely a singular notion of what the party is all about. The concern with democratic control – or, rather, the injured assertion that the party is not truly democratic – arises periodically within the party. Sometimes, as in the case of Mr Tony Benn, the cry is raised in order to imply that the crier understands what the party really wants. The implicit premiss is that if he were made leader he would actually listen to the party. More typically, it is the rallying call of those who are, at the moment, out of favour with the trade union leadership. The block votes which these leaders command at annual conference give them the power to control the conference. This power is said to be undemocratic. In the later 1950s it was the cry of the Bevanite left; today it is heard from the European right. McKenzie is, in effect, agreeing with those who criticise the system as undemocratic. This is to take these rallying cries too literally. It is also to think of the party (and especially annual conference) as a policy-making machine.

Professor Miliband, in *Parliamentary Socialism*, has an entirely different attitude to the party. He sees the history of the party, which he takes to be the history of the party in Parliament, to be a series of betrayals of the true revolutionary consciousness of the working class. *Parliamentary Socialism*, despite its clear moral preference for the ideas of the movement as a whole, is entirely about the ideas and actions of its leaders. Thus, it shares with the McKenzie thesis the notion that the ideology is the ideology of the leadership and that it is a kind of doctrine. Miliband argues that in becoming parliamentary, in agreeing to fight out the class-struggle within the norms of the enemy's system, it has become part of that system: 'The Labour party has not only been a parliamentary party, it has been a party deeply imbued with parliamentarianism.'[6]

Miliband's thesis derives its (considerable) moral force from the unargued and, so far as can reasonably be seen, untrue assertion that there was a revolutionary working-class consciousness to be betrayed. Despite this, it has much to commend it. He observes that Labour leaders have behaved as they have because they have chosen to accept a particular ideology. They could have chosen to reject parliamentary methods altogether or, in 1924 and 1929, they could have refused to assume power without a parliamentary majority. Such a stance would clearly have been quite sensible in 1924 and 1929, and certainly in the latter case would have made a great difference to the history of the party. Yet it is not as clear as Miliband would have us believe that following the parliamentary path need have led to disaster. Neither is it clear that the alternatives would have led to a better result. Surely it is possible to argue that at least part of the problem of the Labour Party has been the ineptness with which it has played the parliamentary game? Skidelsky makes a powerful case that this was part of the trouble with the 1929–31 government. Miliband's emphasis on Labour's acceptance of parliamentary conventions is interesting in additional ways. First, because Labour's acceptance of the conventions of British society and government goes much deeper than that. The party has accepted the notion that the army is a neutral force. Despite provocations by the Conservatives (in Ireland) it has never tried to turn the army or the police into a socialist force even though at several times and in several places it might have tried. It made no capital out of the Invergordon mutiny over sailors' pay or police strikes in Liverpool. It has further accepted – almost without demur – that the local authorities which it controls ought to act within the law, even when that law has been passed by a Conservative government and is opposed by Labour policy and public opinion. The few exceptions to this rule – George Lansbury's refusal to cut unemployment benefit (then a local-authority responsibility) in Poplar and the more recent refusal of Labour councillors in Clay Cross to implement the Housing Finance Act – are exceptions which point to the rule. Both actions embarrassed the national party leaders at the time. Both Liberals and Conservatives have given ample precedents for encouraging local authorities, at the very least, not to implement legislation, but Labour has preferred to be conventional and respectable.

Labour is a very respectable party. Its acceptance, only now being challenged, of the power and method of appointment of judges is another example of how respectable it is. Acceptance of parliamentary conventions and constraints – the thing which worries Miliband – is, surely, less than surprising given the party's general acceptance of all normal conventions. On the contrary, acceptance of parliamentary conventions makes good sense for the Labour Party since Parliament (or, at any rate, the House of Commons) is one powerful institution which Labour can reasonably expect, from time to time, to control.

Miliband's emphasis on Labour's parliamentarianism is also interesting because this acceptance has been accompanied by not a little suspicion in the Labour movement each time Labour has been in office (I will develop this point more fully in Chapter 5). Miliband's book – and this surely is the reason for its popular success – articulates and gives academic authority to this suspicion. It is, that is to say, a successful attempt to mobilise part of the ethos of the movement against the party; or, at any rate, against its present leadership. In other words *Parliamentary Socialism* plays on the ethos of the movement while failing to see that, in other respects, this very ethos has been largely responsible for inspiring the actions it deplores.

Be this as it may, Miliband is surely right to argue that the parliamentary leadership acts under real doctrinal constraints. His common ground with McKenzie is the assumption that these doctrines are the whole of the picture.[7] This assumption is also shared by Professor Beer. Beer sees the Conservative and Labour parties as similar devices – machines for the aggregation of votes and the turning of these votes into parliamentary majorities – with different aims derived from different views of society.

But the Tory belief in economic and social inequality put a fundamental principle between them and Labour. For however ambiguous Labour's commitment to the utopian goal of fellowship had become, British Socialism was at least 'about equality'.[8]

With Miliband, but against McKenzie, Beer sees ideology as a real force controlling political action. With Miliband, too, he sees ideology as a doctrine: it points to a goal and directs towards it.

It is worth noting that all of these books were published in, and partly shaped by the concerns of, the long period of Tory rule, the 'Thirteen Wasted Years' which followed the exhaustion of Labour in 1951. The terms of debate (about the Labour Party, at least) seem to be dictated largely by the polemics between the Bevanites and the Gaitskellites. The electoral failures of a party which purported to represent the overwhelming majority of the electorate provided the background. The failure of nerve of the 1945–51 Labour government towards the end of its term of office was the *leitmotif*. McKenzie and Beer, in effect, took Gaitskell's part. McKenzie argued that oligarchy was both an organisational necessity and a historical feature of the Labour Party, so that the Bevanite attack on it was quixotic. Beer, in so far as he was concerned with the Labour Party, reiterated and elaborated Gaitskell's famous attack on 'Clause 4' (nationalisation of the means of production and distribution) delivered to the 1959 Blackpool annual conference.

For Beer and Gaitskell the way to a Labour majority was through an appeal to middle-class voters, and that appeal required dropping the supposedly frightening baggage of specifically working-class demands – most especially nationalisation. This change of programme was given added political weight by the assumption at the time that large sections of the working class had come to share the middle-class ethos. This fear was mentioned by Gaitskell in his 1959 speech. The notion was that the increasingly affluent workers who owned cars and fridges and went for holidays in Majorca would start to save money, own their own homes and vote Conservative.[9] In the light of this supposed change of values, Gaitskell urged the party to water down its doctrine.

Ironically, Miliband accepted the strength of his argument. The moral tale of his book was addressed to the 'Labour left' – those socialists (the Bevanites presumably) who still thought they could work from within the party. What the Labour left did not see, according to Miliband, was that Gaitskell was right. A parliamentary Labour party needed a watered-down programme to attract middle-class support. Hence the Labour left could pursue its interests only through other channels. In other words, the Bevanite position was quixotic to Miliband, too; but for the different reason that the Labour left ought to leave the parliamentary party because it could never reasonably hope to control it.

Leo Panitch's interesting modifications to Miliband's ideas arose from the different historical circumstances of the collapse of the Wilson government (1964–70). In particular, the clash between the unions and the government, in which the government attempted to introduce legal sanctions against the unions, in a way one attraction of which was the appeasement of middle-class fears of union power, affected Panitch. He argues that there is a conflict between the party as defender of the unions and the party as integrator of the unions into the establishment. It cannot be partisan and judge. He asserts that the party, especially its parliamentary leaders (but also its trade union leaders) tend to opt for the 'integration' function. Rather than defend the special interests of their own people, they try to integrate their people into the establishment. He writes: '. . . the effective ideology of the Labour party was that which stressed the society's coherence and denied its cleavages'.[10] Following Miliband, he sees a fundamental betrayal within this choice.

Panitch's analysis marks an important advance in the writings about the ideology of the Labour Party in so far as he opens up conceptual space for the distinction between the ethos (defending one's own) and the doctrine (producing a classless consensus on the establishment's terms). Unfortunately, he does not follow this up. On the contrary, he immediately closes the space by the assertion that the party always chooses the integration policy and thus betrays the ethos of its supporters.

This, fundamentally, is the position which Panitch later elaborated in his book *Social Democracy and Industrial Militancy: The Labour Party, the Trade Unions and Incomes Policy 1945–1974.*[11] It is similar in essentials to that taken up by David Coates in his book *The Labour Party and the Struggle for Socialism.*[12] Coates and Panitch distinguish themselves from the position taken up by Miliband by their greater explicitness about the revolutionary socialist tradition which they assert the Labour Party to have betrayed. This gives their works a sharpness which Miliband's more subtle account lacks. But the underlying inadequacies are similar in all three accounts save that Panitch and Coates extend their analysis to cover events up to 1974.

The Anderson and Nairn papers were published at a moment of optimism within the socialist movement just before the 1964 election. Where the other writers wonder 'Must Labour lose?' Anderson and Nairn know that Labour can win, and reflect on what can be expected of the new government. In the light of this change in mood, they ask different questions from the others. The question is not 'Must Labour lose?' but 'What will Labour do?'. In order to find the answer they turn back from the history of the party into the history of the working class which produces the party. This provides them with a historical and sociological perspective from which they make a number of important observations.

They posit a British working class that has been generally characterised by an inward-looking and defeatist ethos. This they contrast to a revolutionary will to dominate. The first view they call 'corporative' and the latter 'hegemonic'. Theirs is a distinction between a group concerned to defend itself and its values in a hostile world and a group intent on imposing its will on others. This is hardly a new observation about the British working class – the ideas used by Anderson and Nairn are familiar from the writings on social stratification; neither are they entirely new to the literature on ideology – their 'corporative/hegemonic' recalls Mannheim's 'ideological/utopian'. The advance here is in applying the categories to the ideology of the Labour Party. This gets them beyond talking about the ideology as if it were merely the plaything of the policy-makers.

At this point, however, their analysis falters. Their ideas do not fit the facts. They assert that the British bourgeoisie, like the working class, lacks the will to govern. Consequently, it has never developed a conceptual system capable of justifying its rule. This, as E. P. Thompson retorted, does rather less than justice to Adam Smith.[13] It also underestimates the courage and resourcefulness of several generations of British trade unionists who struggled time and again to assert their will against their employers. Undeterred by this, Anderson and Nairn blame the philosophical vacuity which they ascribe to British socialism on the philosophical vacuity of British capitalism. Without a self-confident philosophy of capitalism to revolt against, British workers have fallen into the trap of emulating the 'empiricism' of their rulers. In other words, like their masters they have failed to set out a coherent analysis of their predicament. In lieu of such an analysis, Anderson and Nairn argue, the Labour Party has welcomed the piecemeal policy-makers of the Fabian Society. But this welcome merely serves to cover the lack of any real ideology; for Anderson and Nairn, the nasty secret of the Labour Party is that it has become parliamentary and consequently does not need – indeed, would now merely be embarrassed by – any revolutionary guide to action. In Parliament the party, according to Anderson, following

8   *Doctrine and Ethos in the Labour Party*

McKenzie and Miliband, is the creature of the government machine. Thus, Anderson sees the 'corporative ideology' of the British workers leading the Labour Party into Parliament where it can find many excuses to take its mind off its ideological weaknesses. The room opened up by raising the question of the character of the working-class ethos and its relation to the doctrine of the Labour Party is thus lost. All these commentaries have an exclusively doctrinal notion of the ideology of the party. When they look for the effect of the ideology they look at its policy-making machine. They look, that is to say, at how it translates its doctrines into policy and how it translates that policy into action. This one-sidedness is perhaps clearest in David Coates's book, for his method is to compare the achievements of each Labour government with the promises made in the manifesto for the election which preceded its return.

With the exception of Professor Beer they do not find that the ideology of the party, thus understood, has made a successful impact on Britain. McKenzie applauds the strength of the constitutional mechanism – he has cabinet government mainly in mind – which has held Labour's socialism in check. Miliband, on the other side, deprecates this state of affairs. Anderson and Nairn, as well as David Coates and Panitch, think that Labour's doctrinal aspirations have been defeated in other ways basically by the strength (variously marshalled) of British capitalism. This exclusively doctrinal view of ideology is unduly restrictive and misses certain important features of the party.

II

In order to open up the ideology of the party to a more satisfactory analysis it is necessary to distinguish between two elements in that ideology: its doctrine and its ethos. What do I mean by doctrine and how does it differ from ethos? A doctrine is a more or less elaborated set of ideas about the character of (in this case) social, economic and political reality which is accepted by a considerable group of people. In the case of political doctrines, these ideas lead to a programme of action, often by being expressed in a series of policies. Doctrines are ideas which have been argued about and agreed by a group of people. Any doctrine or part of a doctrine is always open to challenge and may be modified if experience shows this to be necessary or prudent. The ideology of the Labour Party contains a number of ideas which are doctrines of this kind. It contains a body of thought about the nature of man, of society and of how they are related. In the case of the Labour Party these doctrines have been derived from diverse sources: from Marx, Morris, Blatchford, Shaw, the Webbs, Orwell, Tawney and Herbert Morrison amongst others. Despite this diversity of sources, there is common doctrinal ground – for example, that men are, in most important senses, fundamentally equal. There is further agreement on the idea that a society which does not treat them as equals or allow each to grow to his full potential is unjust. It has reached some agreement on a series of policies – progressive taxation, comprehensive state education, free medical care, state intervention in the economy – designed to bring about a more equal Britain. An important feature of this doctrinal aspect of the ideology of the party is that it is open to all who believe it. Indeed, the doctrines of the party are partly designed with an eye to attracting new elements into the party. When the Liberal Party was breaking up in the 1920s some members of that party were attracted to Labour because of Labour's belief in internationalism and pacificism (the party no longer believes in these things). In a later era the party's anti-imperialism won its converts. One question we may ask about the contemporary Labour Party is whether its current doctrines attract or repel potential new supporters.

This openness is worth stressing – and not simply because Labour (like all parties) always needs converts, but because openness to conversion is a feature of the doctrinal dimension of an ideology. There is nothing about a doctrine which confines belief in it to those who have long been acquainted with it; neither is it the case that doctrines can appeal only to those who stand to gain by them. This openness is particularly important to a party which by name, tradition and, indeed, doctrine works on behalf of one section of society: the working class. Labour gets the overwhelming majority of its support from people who consider themselves workers, but it also gets a more or less constant one-sixth of its vote from others.[14] Its ability to form a government has always depended on its ability to win votes from what Herbert Morrison called 'the little-man'. To win and keep this support from non-working-class people it needs doctrines which appeal to them.

But Labour's ideology has another dimension. Its ideology is also an expression of the ethos of the dominant group in the party. It incorporates sets of values which spring from the experience of the British working class. Typically, these values affect personal relationships. Loyalty to an elected leader is one such. They affect also relations with other groups, with society as a whole and with its political agents, and they reflect the role of the working class in the United Kingdom.

There is a close connection between an ethos, as I understand it, and the experience of the people whom it characterises. An ethos arises out of an experience – in the case of the British working class, out of an experience of exploitation. People who are exploited need ways of dealing with their exploiters. This should not be taken to imply, as sometimes I think it is, that all those who have been exploited are likely to react similarly. Far from it. Different people and different groups of people react to their various experiences in a wide variety of ways. This has certainly been the case in Britain. Different parts of the working class have had different reactions to their experiences. Some have reacted to exploitation by deference, others by revolt, and still others by combining in self-defence.[15] A discussion of the ethos of the 'labour aristocrats' illustrates this point.

Professor Hobsbawm locates a strong, more or less self-conscious and powerful labour aristocracy in Britain in the period between 1840 and 1890.[16] They were noticeably better paid and better organised than the proletariat properly speaking. They generally possessed special skills which they jealously kept to themselves. Marx and Engels noted the existence of such a group and were concerned about the conservative, inward-looking ethos of it. Their main concern seems to have been to keep themselves above the rest of the working class. In Marx and Engels' description, which Hobsbawm largely supports, the ethos of the group was defensive. They were stout upholders of the general order of society. This interpretation has recently been challenged by Pelling and Hinton.[17] Speaking about individual members of the labour aristocracy in a later period, Pelling and Hinton point out that they were very much the vanguard of socialism. There is no contradiction here. In the period which led up to the First World War the position which the labour aristocrats occupied was being challenged by new machinery (which rendered their skills superfluous) and by dilution of their ranks with unskilled workers. The response to the challenge varied. Some became socialist, even revolutionary, while others (usually the official leaders of the unions) became more conservative, even reactionary. But the variety of these reactions to the experience of exploitation should not blind us to its over-riding similarity when these reactions are compared with those of people who have different experiences. However variously labour aristocrats – or the entire working class, for that matter – reacted, all of their reactions are readily distinguishable from those of middle-class groups.

But over-riding similarity, or diverse reactions, one thing which distinguishes an ethos sharply from a doctrine is that the former is not open to recruitment by agreement. It is one thing for the intellectual members of the Labour movement to seek to understand, and to be sympathetic to, the ethos of the workers. Their understanding, however sympathetic, cannot have the same meaning to them that it has to those for whom it arises naturally out of experience.

It is not surprising that those who have commented on Labour's ideology should have concentrated their attention on the doctrinal dimension of that ideology. Issuing, challenging, refuting, elaborating doctrines is, after all, one of the characteristic occupations of intellectuals. Their emphasis on doctrine is explicable as an emphasis on what they know about. It would be very unfortunate, however, for me to give the impression that my distinction between doctrine and ethos is an expression of the distinction between intellectuals and workers; that doctrines are the characteristic way intellectuals think and that workers are at the less demanding, less articulate level of ethos. Intellectuals do like playing with doctrines, and are at home in doctrinal disputes, but they have an ethos every bit as constraining as the workers'. I emphasise the workers' ethos here for political reasons. The Labour Party – not the Fabian Society – is my subject. The centre of gravity in the Labour Party is located in working-class institutions – overwhelmingly in the trade unions. The party allows middle-class intellectuals (of both right and left) to give voice to its ideas, but there can be little doubt as to whose ideas we hear. Of course, the ethos around which the Labour Party is built is different from the middle-class ethos common in the Liberal and Conservative parties. Labour's distinctive background gives rise to distinctive practices and institutions. If Labour's ethos were similar to the other parties', her practices (such as tenderness to her leaders) might well also have been similar, too, and the importance of the ethos might have remained unnoticed.

III

Those who think of Labour's ideology mainly in terms of doctrinal commitment have a number of advantages over me in arguing their thesis. In the first place they can point to specific evidence about Labour's doctrine. Evidence can be found in resolutions sent by constituency parties to annual conference, in resolutions passed at annual conference, in policy documents issued by Transport House and other, less official bodies, and in the party's manifestos. This evidence is abundant and has been regularly produced, so that it is possible to trace different influences on party doctrines (and policies) and trace changes in them over time. Another advantage which those who interpret ideology as doctrine possess is that they can argue from this evidence about the effect of their subject. We can look, say, at the history of the argument for comprehensive secondary education, or for full employment; we can see the extent to which Labour has any claim to be the effective proponent of these policies and we can look at the difference the adoption of these policies by government has made.

The fact that the doctrinaires are articulate gives those who would write their histories obvious purchase. We find the doctrine in the closely argued tracts of the Fabians, the Tribune Group and others. There are few such sources for the ethos. The ethos derives from working-class experience. The problem in discussing this experience is that, even today, we know relatively little about it. For this reason it is necessary to bring to the reader's attention the fact that the observations which follow are largely speculative and are based on slim material. When describing the ethos of a group we are forced to make hypotheses on the basis of the footprints which the group has left behind. All this makes the ethos more difficult than the doctrine to investigate – but not for that reason any less real or less important. I propose in this section to try to overcome these difficulties by pointing to four features of the Labour Party which are odd in the sense that their existence could not be accounted for if the party were the simple vote-getting, policy-making machine it is normally assumed to be. In each case the feature I will point to will distinguish Labour from other parties. In each case I will suggest that the practice is traceable to, or clearly consonant with, some aspect of pre-existing working-class practice or ethos.

The first feature I have already mentioned and discussed: Labour is reluctant to sack its leaders. This point can be rephrased. Labour is loyal to those who serve it. This loyalty is not often cross-cut by a demand for efficiency or effectiveness. The notion that a leader is meant to *do* something is overwhelmed by the sense that we must hang together. This strong sense of loyalty to those who have jobs is related in obvious ways to the experience of protecting employment. Too often the cry for 'increased efficiency' has been just a cover for doing some of our boys out of their jobs.

'Loyalty' in the sense of loyalty to leaders, or in the sense of loyalty to the friends and familiar faces of one's past, is strong in the party. Loyalty in this sense requires long acquaintance and presumes a comfortable relationship with known surroundings and practices. Such an attitude is hardly compatible with the astringent demands of revolutionary struggle. One does not normally revolt against comfortable habits. A group loyal to its established leaders lack a revolutionary ethos.

Loyalty to the movement comes into the party through the trade unions and even further back through the friendly societies. Many British unions began as friendly societies. Even today the banners of these unions bear slogans proclaiming 'Fraternity and Brotherhood'. The societies strengthened their members by uniting them. In a world in which the bosses used a man when they needed him and tossed him aside when he was inconvenient, the friendly societies protected their members (and their families) in adversity. The bosses always knew they could divide and rule; the men learned to stick together and trust one another. In unity there was strength. This was the very antithesis of individualism. In a literal sense, it was socialism. The lesson was clear: so long as the class was united the men were strong. It is a lesson which has been institutionalised in the Labour Party and the trade unions.

G. D. H. Cole seems to have been particularly sensitive to loyalty and alive to its importance in the Labour Party. In separate places he attributed Arthur Henderson's success to his loyalty and Oswald Mosley's failure to his disloyalty. Cole's opinion of 'Uncle Arthur' is worth quoting at length:

> . . . not a particularly clever man, or an inspiring speaker. He had neither the glamour of MacDonald nor the incisiveness of Snowden, nor the human warmth of George Lansbury. But he had great qualities – honesty, absence of self-seeking, doggedness and patience in action, and faith in the ethical ideals of justice and freedom. . . . He never let a colleague down, or attempted to shift to other men's shoulders the burden of his own mistakes. 'Uncle Arthur', as he was commonly called, made the Labour party what it was. . . . Whatever he made it, he made it for the common people and not for himself.[18]

This emphasis on loyalty within the movement has been variously received. Miliband, somewhat uncomfortably, suggests that this strong demand for loyalty has always put the left at a disadvantage when they felt a need to criticise the party leaders.[19] From a diametrically opposed point of view the historian of revisionism, Haseler, relates with considerable relief that loyalty kept the party from splitting up when its right-wing leadership could invent only the thinnest of doctrinaire theses for their revision of British socialism.[20] Studies of Labour constituency parties point to a similar trait operating at this level: debate about policy issues is often inhibited by loyalty to the leaders.[21] The value of this loyalty to the leadership is difficult to over-estimate. Their position is strengthened beyond what doctrine or formal power would allow. Hugh Dalton, to cite an authority very different from G. D. H. Cole, observed that office-holders in the Labour movement had a strong sense of 'social security'.[22] They knew they could depend on their followers to return them – often unopposed – to office.

It should be noted that the Conservative Party, too, makes much of its 'loyalty' – but Conservatives have something entirely different in mind when making this claim. For them loyalty means having one's arguments in the privacy of the party's inner councils and keeping one's mouth shut in public. This kind of loyalty is also easily related to an ethos – in this case, that of a ruling class. Loyalty thus understood restricts effective decision making to those few on the inside. A number of the conventions of the British constitution, such as the collective responsibility of the Cabinet for all its decisions, are also predicated on the same ethos. It works just so long as all Cabinet members agree to play the game by these rules. It is perhaps no accident that Labour Cabinets have difficulty operating this collective responsibility. They have much more difficulty than Conservative Cabinets in keeping their discussions out of the press. Loyalty in the Conservative ethos has little enough to do with leadership selection and support: 'oligarchy tempered by assassination' is more to the point.

The second feature of the party which can be ascribed to its ethos concerns personal style. The Labour Party expects sacrifice from its leaders and employees. It pays its employees shockingly badly. In 1951, Labour had 296 full-time agents working for constituency parties; by 1973 the number had fallen to 130. In that year agents were paid on a scale which rose from £1,530 to a princely £2,070. The top rate was half of an MP's salary at the time and, more to the point, about equal to the wage of the average male manual worker.

It is perhaps reasonable to expect a party which embraces the doctrine of equality to pay its employees the average manual wage. What is more impressive is the opprobrium which attaches to some in the party who too openly flaunt a middle-class salary or education. Vulgar success is not objected to – anyone can strike it rich – it is cool self-assurance that raises hackles. This objection is raised particularly against smooth, obviously well-educated right-wingers. Mr Tony Benn, son of a peer, is forgiven his Oxford manner for he is a solid man of the left. Mr Roy Jenkins was always held in suspicion by large groups in the party because he combined right-wing politics with an inability to pronounce the letter 'r'. One thing one had to admire about Mr Jenkins was his absolute refusal to compromise his style. In the 1976 leadership contest he allowed himself to be interviewed by television cameramen while playing tennis on his own grass court. He lost the contest, too. Badly.

The Healeys, Callaghans and Crossmans with their country estates sail close to the wind; Robens, Chalfont, Shawcross, Taverne and Maxwell all did well enough from the party, but are now held in contempt, and used as a reason for suspecting others on the right, because of their apparent affluence. Doing well and acquiring a 'Tory-like' style of living are resented more than corruption. It is not so much a question of making, or even inheriting, money, as a question of social superiority. Corrupt Labour councillors and affluent left-wingers do not offend the ethos.[23] The former are forced to keep in touch, to buy the boys the occasional round of drinks – if nothing else – to retain their source of wealth. The latter also need to keep in touch with their source of power. The problem with the others – of whom Roy Jenkins was long the epitome – is that they are thought to use their supporters' votes in order to enable them to behave like Tories. They made no sacrifice to a movement largely made up of people who see themselves as exploited.

These constraints are easily enough manipulated by the sophisticated. Harold Wilson always knew precisely when to reacquire his northern accent.[24] I have seen a much-loved figure on the left of the party travel the last few hundred yards to a public meeting on foot, haversack on back. The ministerial car waited round the corner. For them such conceits are harmless enough. It is also true that others (Callaghan, Lever, Crossman, Crosland) have not found personal wealth a bar to advancement within the party. Perhaps the most one can say is that such a style is taken to be a mark against a Labour politician. In tight situations such marks can matter. Of course, the accumulation of private wealth runs counter not only to the party's ethos, but also to its professed doctrine. This doctrine I will consider in Chapter 3.

The third feature of the party which relates to its ethos is its peculiar attitude to money. It has an attitude to its own finances which would win approval from Samuel Smiles himself.[25] Labour saves. Indeed, nowhere does the Labour Party more clearly reveal its origins in the trade unions, and beyond them in the friendly societies and insurance clubs of Victorian Britain, than in its attitudes to its own money.[26]

There are a number of manifestations of this. Perhaps the most dramatic evidence of it is to be found in its use of its general election fund. This account (controlled by the National Executive Committee) actually grew at every election from 1945 to 1966. It would have grown in 1970, too, but for the fact that some of the hoard (£150,000 of a total £402,000) was used to pay the salaries of additional agents. The fact is that the amount of money spent on every general election between 1945 and 1974 was less than the amount of money collected for that campaign. When one considers how impoverished Labour's constituencies are this is madness. These funds could be regularly used to pay agents' salaries (incidentally increasing NEC control of the party). They are not spent; the money is simply hoarded.

Professor Rose has recently shown that the party – and the unions – regularly build up contingency funds for emergencies which are far larger than prudence alone dictates.[27] Rose cites other examples of this practice. The unions hold political funds in reserve. The amount of these funds has grown regularly. In 1959 the reserve was £1,234,000. The figure rose to £1,703,000 in 1970. By 1970 the total held in reserve was $1\frac{2}{3}$ that normally collected in a year.

The deposit insurance fund provides another example of economically irrational saving. The fee for a lost deposit (£150) could be paid sixty-nine times out of the 1970 fund of £10,418. It did, in fact, decrease in 1974 with its two general elections but still stood at £6,970. Each constituency party subscribes £10 to the fund for an insurance policy against having to pay for a lost deposit. It's a small thing, no doubt, but £2.50 per election would do amply. The same principle applies to the by-election insurance funds. In fact, the party transfers some of its reserve hoards to make up deficits of annual expenditure. Rose aptly notes: 'Labour finance reflects a particular state of mind more than a lack of cash in the bank.'[28]

Another interesting financial practice of the Labour Party is its method of dues collection. Annual memberhip of the party now costs £1.20. Pensioners pay less. For years the regular practice was for party activists to call at each member's home once a month and collect one-twelfth of the annual subscription. The membership card still gives over one side to a subscription grid. There are three columns – 'date', 'amount' and 'received by' – and twelve spaces under each. Each member's card was marked up each month by the local activist who called to collect his subscription. In this way an important face-to-face bond between the more active members and the more passive ones cound be maintained and all could be kept in touch with what was happening in the party.

As a way of keeping the party together, then, the practice of collecting monthly subscriptions might have its point. But as a way of collecting money it is absurd. The amount paid each month is less than the cost of an average bus-ride. It is less than the price of a pint of milk. The time expended in collecting money in this way is grossly disproportionate to the amount collected. This practice of monthly payments began long ago and can be accounted for by the relative poverty of the people who built the Labour Party. Its continued existence cannot be entirely explained in this way. The subscription is still small, and still payable on a monthly basis, partly because that is the way it has always been. But there is another reason. Those members of constituency and ward parties who collect the subscriptions and organise jumble sales, whist drives and small lotteries to raise money use the time and energy they spend as a kind of political weapon. They are able to argue at local meetings that 'We must spend more time raising money and less time writing fancy resolutions'. No organisation which wishes to contest future elections can allow itself to go bankrupt; and since other methods of money raising, such as paying subscriptions by banker's order, are firmly castigated as middle class the local parties have to listen to those willing to work at money raising. My experience (in a Labour-held seat in the centre of a university town) is that those who marshal the 'money-collecting' argument tend to be opposed to the usually younger, more policy-oriented, often Trotskyist, members. The opposition between these two groups is often seen as a clash of doctrines alone; of the party's right and its left. It is better seen as a clash between those, the younger members, who think out their attitudes in doctrinal terms and those who do not. (This is not said in an attempt to justify the stand of either side. I shall argue in the last chapter that both are standing on rapidly melting ice.) Labour's practices with its own money cannot be understood as the result of any financial doctrines whatever. They are simply practices handed down from generations of thrifty working people.

The fourth feature of the Labour Party's practices which can be attributed to its ethos, and the last one I shall mention – for I hope my general point about the impact of the ethos on the behaviour of the party is now taken – is its belief in formal explicit rules. For just about every level of the party there is a written formal 'rule-book' procedure. This is not so in the other parties, though they now show some signs of moving in Labour's direction. The Conservative Party has proceeded until very recently largely on the basis of accepted practice rather than formal rules. Its change in the direction of Labour's procedure does not indicate a late conversion to the working-class ethos, simply a general loss of nerve and sense of direction and consequent grasping at any available alternative to its past procedures. The selection of leaders is a case in point. Labour uses the 'exhaustive ballot' method with a rigidly defined electorate – the Parliamentary Labour Party. Until the selection of Mr Heath in 1965 the Conservative leaders simply emerged and were in time replaced. Labour's procedure was explicit to the extent of laying it down that the leader could only be elected once a year (at the beginning of the parliamentary session). He was safe for the other 364 days of the year. A Tory leader could be asked to go at any time.

The 'rule-book' is not, of course, slavishly followed. If it were, much of my thesis about the impact of the working-class ethos would fall, but it is always there to be invoked in case of a dispute. This is much like the position in trade unions and co-operative societies. Many of them have hideously complicated rule-books; most of them work, most of the time, by agreed practice within the spirit of the rules. Formal rules are a way of at once licensing leaders and trying to constrain them. A group of people who have had to fight their way to acceptance, and for whom the normal legal rules and customary practices of the ruling classes are alien, has need of its own self-contained quasi-legal rule-system. It is this experience of being excluded and exploited which led working people to create their own institutions and endow them with their own formal structures. This experience and the resulting practice have been passed on to the Labour Party.

It might be objected that Labour has to have a formal written constitution because the party has a federal structure, but this is to confuse the result with the process which makes it possible. The Conservative Party with its associated National Union (the party in the country), 1922 Committee (back-benchers), Central Office and Research Department is not less complicated than the Labour Party. It does not, however, formalise the relationship between the parts: much more weight is given to the decisions of the leader. He (or she) has considerable freedom (and patronage) to reorganise the party structure.

In these four important respects the activities of the party, on all levels, are influenced by the ethos of the people from whom it springs.

This ethos should thus be an important part of what we have in mind when we analyse the party's ideology.

IV

One must, I think, take seriously the claim that the party is part of a movement. The word 'movement' can be taken in the full force given to it by Donald Schon.[29] A movement is a collection of loosely related institutions and individuals all working for a vaguely defined common goal. A movement differs from an institution.

The members of the movement expect to make sacrifices for the whole and expect their fellows to do the same. One notices how the various outside bodies affiliated to the Labour Party contribute to it at various levels. There is no one command structure but several. Anyone defeated in election to one level of the party – say, the constituency – can very often get up by a different route. The party is therefore not a coherent whole. To take the extreme contrast (on paper), observe an army. If the party were more like an army, the difference between its doctrine and its ethos might not be of much concern. The doctrine of the chiefs of staff would be the doctrine of the whole. Each member of the party would act in accordance with it. 'Commands' would come down and information would, given a little luck, go up. Each man would have an assigned place given to him by the party. This is not the case in the Labour Party. It is hardly the case in many parties, except some tightly organised revolutionary cells. This means that one must exercise some care in speaking of the relationship between the various parts of the party and of the parts of the ideology which characterise them.

The party acts in different ways in wards and constituencies from the way it behaves nationally in Parliament. The socialist societies behave differently from the constituencies. The trade unions have expectations different from those of the officers in Transport House. Consequently, one cannot deduce the character of one part in any simple way from an examination, however detailed, of another. In the light of this, the all but exclusive emphasis on the parliamentary party and the annual conference in the literature is misleading.

Were the Labour Party a parliamentary grouping united by interest or disposition to which a mass party base was added – as is the case in the Tory Party and in Ostrogorski's 'party' – its doctrine might be the whole of its ideology. But this is most emphatically not what the Labour Party is. It was formed to defend in Parliament the interests of already existing institutions. Its success in its early years was ensured by the Taff Vale decision in which the courts changed the interpretation of the law against the interests of the unions. It is reasonable to speculate that had it not been for this attack on the working class, an attack which could only be repelled (short of revolution) by parliamentary action, the Labour Representation Committee (as it then was) might have disappeared like so many socialist groupings before it. The model followed by the party leadership in those early days was much more the Parnellite Irish Party than either the governing Liberal or Tory parties. The LRC was a defensive pressure-group, not a serious challenger for power. One of its architects, Keir Hardie, even toyed (in public) with the notion of forming a new national grouping under Lloyd George's leadership.[30] This was hardly the action of a would-be Prime Minister.

Undoubtedly the party changed character in 1918 when it adopted a new constitution and became committed to forming a government. But to pretend that the policy-makers, the intellectuals and the leadership were in command from that moment is simply absurd. In a sense this pretence is a form of 'intellectual MacDonaldism'. Where 'MacDonaldism' consists in the betrayal of the needs of the movement for personal position, the 'doctrine' commentators betray the party in a more subtle and more fundamental way. They ignore the feelings which cement together the people in the party: the feelings which make it worth working for and voting for.

Undoubtedly, too, the party has been changing its character in important ways since 1945. Since then its leaders, as ministers, have had the experience of power. This experience has introduced a new element into the party. Before 1945 ideologists within the party had frequently invoked the 'levers of power' metaphor to justify the effort required to support the party. Work for the party, the argument went, and we will some day be able to grasp the levers of power. Now the party had men with their hands on these levers – or so it seemed. The arguments in favour of supporting the party could never be so simple again. This experience also modified the expectations which people might reasonably have of the party. Yet no such modification is important enough to weaken the central point: the dominant groups in the movement are the various parts of the working class. It is to them we must turn.

Rodney Barker, in his study of the Labour Party's policy on education, makes what seems to me the essential point. 'The Labour party', he says, 'derived its ambitions not from political principles, nor from broad visions of a different society, but from the social and economic opportunities of which its working-class members had experience.'[31] The emphasis needs to be put exactly where Barker puts it, on the political experience and expectations of the working class.

The experience of that class can be summed up, for brevity's sake, in two aspects: exploitation by outsiders, and the slow, painful building of its own defensive organisations. That it was exploited by the owners of capital is not in need of emphasis or elaboration. Indeed, the only surprising thing is how long this concept took to sink in. Robert Roberts remarks of his own childhood in a Salford slum:

> The class struggle, as manual workers in general knew it, was apolitical and had place entirely within their own society. . . . All in all it was a struggle against the fates, and each family fought it out as best it could. Marxist 'ranters' from the [Hyndham] Hall . . . paid fleeting visits to our street and insisted that we, the proletariat, stood locked in a titanic struggle with some wicked master class. . . . Most people passed by. . . .[32]

That manual workers were also exploited by the government is not sufficiently recognised or taken seriously enough. Surely the whole weight of the 'ideology as doctrine' position is based on the assumption that the party of the working class saw government as a class-neutral instrument presently held by their enemies which could be captured and used to the ends of the workers. This may be how Ramsay MacDonald and Keir Hardie came to see it, but if we are talking about the mass of workers at the turn of the century – and for some time thereafter – this was simply not how government was seen. The experience of government was of oppression in general and humiliation in particular. The operation of the Poor Law – which humbled able-bodied people in distress – was widely resented. The progressive legislation of the last twenty years of the nineteenth century, even where it was intended to improve the lives of the poor, was widely suspected and distrusted by its supposed beneficiaries. As Pelling points out, 'the most popular leader among the working class was Gladstone, and he was more hostile than almost anyone else to the extension of the power of the state'.[33] Such an experience does not easily lead to the production of legislative manifestos. It is not a likely foundation for the kind of reformist platforms on which Labour politicians have readily stood. Such platforms must be fashioned by men with a different background.

One result of such an experience of exploitation is a relatively low level of interest in politics as such. Politics was, after all, a game played almost entirely in private by a small number of wealthy and remote families – rather like merchant banking today. Collectively, the decisions of merchant bankers have no little influence on our society, yet I suggest that few of us have the remotest idea of how they are made. Neither do we spend much time worrying about it. Why, then, is it surprising that working men, so much further removed from access to power and information than we, did not waste time writing, say, *Labour and the New Social Order*? Even today one cannot help but notice how little space the popular press gives to politics – and most of that space is devoted to personalities and scandal. Conversely, there are no socialist daily newspapers in Britain (or any Western country that I know of) which can support themselves financially. The *Daily Herald*, despite subsidies, collapsed under the weight of politics.[34] This sceptical attitude is illustrated by Hoggart's observation that working people think of politicians as fiddlers: 'E's a real political all right,' they say, meaning that he is 'all talk and no do', and that 'such as 'ein never really do owt for people like us'.[35] Roberts observes: 'Having no official connection with national government beyond an occasional election, they did not feel the state as a reality at all.'[36]

Given this kind of background, it is not the least surprising that the ethos of the party is 'defensive'. Many in the Labour Party do not expect to be in power and are, as C. A. R. Crosland observed, distinctly uncomfortable at the achievement when they make it.[37] Ernest Bevin, who knew that attitude well, hated it. He once told an audience of dockers:

Before our movement developed . . . you responded to the whip: I want you to respond to the call of liberty. . . . There are ninety-nine per cent of the men and women in this audience tonight who believe they are of a lower order than the other class. You accept it, and I want to get rid of it.[38]

Bevin's biographer observes that Bevin saw very clearly that, if working men were to achieve anything, they had to 'overcome the lack of confidence in themselves'.[39] One can but sympathise at the annoyance this attitude must cause would-be Labour leaders; but at the same time one cannot help wondering if the Labour Party could long survive the change in social conditions which would be necessary to end it. Would a genuinely self-confident working class put up with the existing Labour Party. It is worth reflecting, too, that this 'loser' attitude is at once a realistic assessment of the position of the workers and of the party they support and, in so far as it is internalised, a remnant of the 'deferential Toryism' in the heart of the Labour Party. This particular piece of Labour's ideology is highly unsuited to a governing party. It prefigures the lack of political grip which has characterised so many Labour administrations and paralysed so many of its leaders.

The 'defensive' character of the movement's ethos is expressed in various ways: it is evident in Labour's touching belief in its manifestos; it is evident in its insistence on treating its own elected representatives as delegates; it is manifest in its loyalty to its leaders; it is evident in all the practices noticed in part III of this chapter, and yet the interesting thing is that this defensiveness has continually been modified. Defensiveness is not submissiveness. The various parts of the working class were, throughout the decades leading up to the formation of the party, forming more and ever stronger institutions. Its leadership, if rarely revolutionary, was often in rebellion. The movement acquired gradually an experience of incremental success through the use of its defensive institutions. The rallying cry of this experience, which at once epitomises and caricatures it, is 'solidarity'.

NOTES

1   McKenzie, R. T., *British Political Parties: the Distribution of Power within the Conservative and Labour Parties*, 2nd ed (London, 1963).
2   Miliband, R., *Parliamentary Socialism* (London, 1961) and Panitch, Leo, 'Ideology and integration: the case of the British Labour Party', *Political Studies*, June 1971.
3   Beer, S. H., *Modern British Politics: A Study of Parties and Pressure Groups* (London, 1965).
4   Nairn, T., 'The nature of the Labour Party 1 and 2', *New Left Review*, nos 27, 28, 1964, and Anderson, P., 'The origins of the present crisis', *New Left Review*, no. 23, 1963.
5   McKenzie, *British Political Parties*, p. 317.
6   Miliband, *Parliamentary Socialism*, p. 13.
7   See, however, ibid. where the mould is very nearly broken.
8   Beer, *Modern British Politics*, p. 387.
9   See an admirable review of the whole discussion in Forester, T., *The Labour Party and the Working Class* (London, 1976), ch. 2.
10 Panitch, 'Ideology and integration', p. 193.
11 Panitch, Leo, *Social Democracy and Industrial Militancy: The Labour Party, The Trade Unions and Incomes Policy 1945–1974* (Cambridge, 1976).
12 Coates, D., *The Labour Party and the Struggle for Socialism* (Cambridge, 1975).
13 Thompson, E. P., 'The peculiarities of the English', in Miliband, R., and Saville, J. (eds.), *The Socialist Register 1965*. See, too, Anderson, P., 'The origins of the present crisis'.
14 Forester, *Labour Party and Working Class*, ch. 2.
15 Useful summaries in Parkin, F., *Class Inequality and Political Order* (London, 1972) and Forester, *Labour Party and Working Class*, ch. 3.
16 Hobsbawm, E. J., 'Labour aristocracy in nineteenth century England', in Saville, J. (ed.), *Democracy and the Labour Movement* (London, 1954), pp. 208ff.
17 Pelling, H., 'The working class and the origins of the welfare state', in *Popular Politics and Society in Late Victorian Britain* (London, 1968), and Hinton, J., *The First Shop Stewards Movement* (London, 1974).
18 Cited in Cole, M., *The Life of G. D. H. Cole* (London, 1970), p. 168.
19 Miliband, *Parliamentary Socialism*, p. 36.
20 Haseler, S., *The Gaitskellites* (London, 1969), p. 6.
21 Janosik, E., *Constituency Labour Parties* (London, 1968), p. 85.
22 Dalton, H., *Call Back Yesterday* (London, 1953), p. 191.
23 See the depressing tale of Eddie Milne. Milne, E., *No Shining Armour* (London, 1976). Milne, who fought corruption, is an exception whose loneliness proves the rule.

24 For an unkind account, see Foot, P., *The Politics of Harold Wilson* (Harmondsworth, 1968); and, for a less critical one, Foot, M., *Harold Wilson: A Pictorial Biography* (London, 1964).
25 See Briggs, A., *Victorian People* (Harmondsworth, 1965), ch. 5.
26 For a general description, see Gosden, P. H. J. H., *Self-Help* (London, 1973).
27 The factual information on this point is all from Rose, R., *The Problem of Party Government* (London, 1974), pp. 239*ff*. This book is a mine of useful information.
28 ibid., p. 242.
29 Schon, D., *Beyond the Stable State* (London, 1971).
30 Bealey, F., and Pelling, H., *Labour and Politics 1900–1906* (London, 1958), p. 145; compare p. 155. This book is a valuable commentary on this period.
31 Barker, R., *Education and Politics 1900–1951* (Oxford, 1972), p. 136.
32 Roberts, R., *The Classic Slum* (Harmondsworth, 1973), p. 28. An excellent book on this subject.
33 Pelling, *Popular Politics*, p. 17.
34 McKibbon, R., 'The evolution of a national party' (unpublished Oxford D.Phil. thesis), Folios 406*ff*.
35 Hoggart, R., *The Uses of Literacy* (Harmondsworth, 1957), p. 280.
36 Roberts, R., *Classic Slum*, p. 163.
37 Crosland, C. A. R., *The Future of Socialism* (London, 1956), p. 123.
38 Cited in Bullock, A., *The Life and Times of Ernest Bevin*, Vol. I (London, 1960), p. 132.
39 ibid.

2
Labour's Ethos:
The Uses of the Past

I

Spokesmen for the Conservative Party proudly proclaim the heritage and pedigree of their party. They show some skill at tracing the many connections between the past, Britain's – or perhaps it is England's – past, the past of the Tory Party, and present Tory goals. A party which calls itself Conservative could hardly do otherwise. As the party which has successfully defended the monarchy, the House of Lords, the Established Church, and the private ownership of land against various attacks, it has some right to its claim.

Lord Hailsham, an eloquent and prominent Conservative spokesman, talks of the 'wisdom of the past' from which Conservatives are proud to learn. He contrasts this disposition to that of those who yearn always to start from scratch. Going further, he claims that politicians of Conservative temperament rarely give themselves over to the political struggle wholeheartedly. As the future Home Secretary, Lord Chancellor and chairman of the Conservative Party put it:

> Conservatives do not believe that political struggle is the most important thing in life. In this they differ from Communists, Socialists, Nazis, Fascists, Social Creditors, and most members of the British Labour Party. The simplest among them prefer fox-hunting – the wisest, religion. To the great majority of Conservatives, religion, art, study, family, country, friends, music, fun, duty, all the joy and riches of existence of which the poor no less than the rich are the indefeasible free-holders, all these are higher in the scale than their handmaiden, the political struggle.[1]

Political struggle provides the means by which an unconservative group might destroy the world Hailsham enjoys. A liking for the past and a distaste for rapid or systematic change lead, not surprisingly, to deprecation of the means of change. Hailsham's Conservative Party, which speaks for and leads on behalf of those for whom fox-hunting is one of the simpler pleasures of life, is in no hurry to cut free from the past. Hailsham's view is, of course, hotly disputed by the reformist wing of the Tory Party.

The Labour Party claims to speak for the exploited; or, more precisely, for those who believe they are exploited and for those who sympathise with them. The thing to do about exploitation, once it is recognised for what it is, is to end it. Ending exploitation is one of the things some spokesmen for the Labour Party have in mind when they assert that Labour is the party of the future. Certainly Labour is a party very conscious of time. It is a party which exists, as a result of certain remembered past actions, to do a particular job now and in the future. Whatever else it is, it is not a gentlemanly party. Though some of its members may desperately desire respectability, they do not play at politics the way gentlemen and true conservatives are meant to hunt foxes or play cricket; they are not in politics for the joy of the game or because they feel some obligation to rule. Rather, the Labour Party entered national politics, as indeed its founders had formed trade unions and co-operative societies, to do a job. This concern with a task leads easily to the mistaken belief that Labour's ideology ought to be entirely directed towards the future, and that to the extent that it is concerned with the past, or is romantically attached to its past it is perverted. I will try in this chapter to correct these impressions.

The Labour Party has and needs a strong sense of its own past and of the past of the Labour movement which produced and sustains it. This sense of its past is so central to its ethos that it plays a crucial role in defining what the party is about to those in it. Labour's sense of her past is, of course, an expression of the past experience of the various parts of the British working class. It is these pasts which dictate that Labour must be a party of the future and what kind of future policies it will tolerate.

When it began the party was not in any way a future-oriented party. Until the end of the First World War it could agree only to form a small parliamentary group to defend the interests of the workers and of their unions. It could agree on no positive programme. It was only at the end of the war, in the light of the collapse of Liberalism in Britain, the success of the Bolshevik project in Russia, the increasing militancy of the shop stewards' movement, the emerging socialism of some of the key unions, and the fear that if Labour did not adopt a programme others would and the movement would pass the party by, that the party could state its project.[2] Before then – indeed, for some years thereafter – it was customary for the chairman of the party to open its annual conference with a speech in which he would, inevitably, 'rededicate the party to the ideals of our founders'. More recently, Harold Wilson reported to the 1966 annual conference that he and his colleagues went to the chapel in the crypt of the House of Commons in October 1964 and again after the victory of 1966 to perform 'a service of re-dedication'.[3] Obeisance to Keir Hardie was usual and the fervour of the re-dedication was in no way diminished by the speaker's inability to name the precise ideals to which he was referring. Of course, the various socialist societies which had been affiliated to the party knew from the beginning that they wanted the party to be committed to socialism. But the unions, who controlled the annual conferences from the beginning, would not agree. In any case the socialists could not agree amongst themselves about the kind of socialism with which they wanted to replace capitalism, nor how to achieve their goal. At the end of the war these differences were submerged as the party articulated a project which was gaining in popularity amongst its potential voters.

The project is announced in Clause 4, No. 4, of the 1918 constitution. By 'project' I mean a will for the replacement of the present order of things, which embodies a conception of the new order. Projects need not be realised either violently or speedily, and if we can cleanse 'revolution' of these two associations (as Raymond Williams does in *The Long Revolution*) we can see that the fulfilment of a project constitutes a revolution. Typically, projects emanate from the experience of oppressed or exploited groups. Irish nationalism was a project which emerged from the experience of English oppression. The project posed a resolution to a situation which was perceived as intolerable. We may expect each project to be appropriate to the situation of the people who espouse it. There is a fittingness about projects; they do not come 'off the peg'. A project is, if I may use a Hegelianism, the negation of a negation. Exploitation is a negation of man's natural freedom, and a project negates that negation.

But not all oppressed or exploited groups evolve projects. Some groups or people merely rebel without knowing what they want to do once they have rebelled. Such rebels lack projects because they lack the imagination or the will, or perhaps the means, to create projects; one thinks of mediaeval peasant revolts, 'Captain Swing', and the riots of American blacks. Rebellion may be violent, for it is akin to rage, but unless it transforms itself into revolution it must inevitably end in exhaustion, for it is blind.[4]

Both projects and rebellions are responses to exploitation which spring from within. They are thus to be distinguished from plans. A plan is positive. It is a proposal. A plan for the alleviation of this or that particular aspect of exploitation is different in important ways from either revolution or rebellion. A plan may be used and re-used with little or no adaptation. Plans are applied in various situations.

Another difference: plans are written by professionals – architects, town planners, economists, social administrators, lawyers, accountants – for application to other people's situations.

Yet, for all these differences, planners and revolutionaries have some things in common and can work together. Both are directed towards the future. In some revolutionary movements – such as British socialism – the planners can provide detailed tactics while the basic drive and goal of the movement arise out of the experience of some sections of the working class. Since 1918 the Labour Party has made use of various planners to provide the details and 'take the minutes' of the movement. Thus, Clause 4 (to use its common short title) was actually written by Sidney Webb. Webb, a planner *par excellence*, was fortunate to be on the spot when the leaders of the movement decided to take on intellectual helpers. In Clause 4 we have an example of a revolutionary statement actually chiselled by a planner:

> To secure for the workers by hand or by brain the full fruits of their industry and the most equitable distribution thereof that may be possible, upon the basis of the common ownership of the means of production, distribution, and exchange, and the best obtainable system of popular administration and control of each industry or service.

This clause is the only part of the constitution where the aim of the party is explicitly stated.

The extent of Webb's influence on this project was not great. The actual words are his, but of itself this tells us little about his influence. J. M. Winter has recently shown that Webb did not even believe the sentiments expressed in Clause 4. He offered two versions, the milder of which was: 'To secure for the producers by hand or brain the full fruits of their industry by the Common Ownership of all Monopolies and essential Raw Materials.'[5] Webb, as Winter shows, had completed a long intellectual journey to arrive at even this mild formulation. He offered the other stronger formulation with its syndicalist overtones to placate the 'wild men', thinking that his preferred form would be accepted. In this case at least, we can safely say that the influence of the planner was small; at best he was drafting what other men wanted to see.

Webb's influence was small, too, in that Clause 4 was so vague as to lead successive generations of ideologists to call for a more definite statement. R. H. Tawney, for example, blamed the failure of the 1929–31 government on its lack of creed:

> The gravest weakness of British Labour is one which it shares with the greater part of the world, outside Russia. . . . It lacks a creed. . . .

It does not achieve what it could, because it does not know what it wants. . . . This weakness is fundamental. If it continues uncorrected, there neither is nor ought to be, a future for the Labour Party.[6]

Having failed through its muddle-headedness in the recent past, the party, Tawney suggested, should learn the lesson and prepare a future for itself. This, he believed, could be done by sharpening up Labour's ideology.

More recently, the same point has been made, from different perspectives, about the failures of the 1964–70 government by Royden Harrison and J. P. Mackintosh. Harrison reaffirms Tawney's stand, adding that the job is to make socialism sufficiently distinct from any ideology which could possibly be acceptable to the City or to the Gnomes of Zürich.[7] Mackintosh argues, to put it briefly, that socialism may be equated with a programme of nationalisation, and that since nationalisation is now irrelevant to our economic difficulties socialism should be jettisoned in favour of a reformist ideology which he calls social democracy. By way of criticising two self-confessed socialists, Mackintosh notes:

This [i.e. their] kind of Socialism is a deeply conservative outlook based upon fear of change; it expects that the inevitable burden of adjusting to modern methods will fall predominantly on the workers so that the first priority is to defend the positions already won by the Labour Movement.[8]

Thus, both left and right agree that Labour's socialism is in constant need of redefinition. It needs redefinition because it was so vague in the first place; but also, as Mackintosh observes, because the world changes and, if Labour is actually to run the country as well as fulfil its historic mission, it must keep the future in mind and not dwell unduly on the past.

II

'Nationalisation': Labour's project is the most sensitive and hotly contested issue in its ideology. It is, indeed, almost the only issue within the ideology. This was not so at the time of the clashes between the Bevanites and Gaitskellites at the end of 1950s and in the early 1960s. At that time debates over defence and foreign affairs were taken at least as seriously as nationalisation. One reason for this change must be Britain's reduced status in the world. It was still possible for Harold Macmillan, in the mid-sixties, to believe he could have a serious influence over American nuclear policy. This is now embarrassing. Britain has no world role. Common Market entry was predicated on this truth: it was the final surrender. In this reduced position Britain's parties do not need to take foreign policy seriously. Certainly the Labour Party does not take it remotely as seriously as it used to. The empty space thus created only serves to point up the importance of the dispute over the ownership of productive resources.

Labour's revisionists want to weaken the party's commitment to Clause 4. Two of their reasons for weakening this commitment relate to their concept of the party as a future-oriented organisation. The revisionists, in the first place, no longer believe that further nationalisation is a necessary prelude to the adoption of efficient national plans. They believe that the private owners of capital will fall into the place allotted to them in such plans. In this belief they are breaking with an earlier generation of socialists of whom John Strachey was characteristic. Strachey saw nationalisation as the way forward to a planned society. For him a programme of nationalisation was forward-looking because he was optimistic that, once accomplished, it would enable the nation's planners to take decisions, confident of the benefits for all. This was a hope which, after the 1945–51 government, the revisionists could not share.

To this consideration they added another which made them think of nationalisation as a thing of the past: they believed that nationalisation was no longer electorally popular and was likely to become positively and increasingly unpopular. They accepted the 'embourgeoisement' thesis. They thought that affluent workers would no longer rally to the old symbols which had been so emotive in the thirties and forties. They were right enough about the unpopularity of nationalisation but wrong to think that this would prove fatal to their electoral chances.

Gaitskell, in his famous speech to the 1959 annual conference (in which he put the revisionists' case) put the point: 'We assumed too readily an instinctive loyalty to Labour which was all the time slowly being gradually eroded.' Putting together the two arguments for thinking nationalisation backward-looking and for wanting the Labour Party to dissociate itself from it, he said, 'Let us remember that we are a party of the future, not of the past; that we must appeal to the young as well as the old – young people who have very little reverence for the past. It is no use waving the banner of a bygone age.'[9] This was a theme picked up by at least one bright-eyed revisionist who followed his leader to the platform. A Mr A. Wedgewood Benn (later Lord Stansgate) seconded Gaitskell by saying: 'You cannot attract and keep the loyalty of younger people, if the majority of the movement are still thinking too much about the past, as they seem to be.'[10]

Any ideology which attaches to an organisation has to face two ways. It must guide policy by posing a concept of what the party is about, and it must provide the party with an ethos which keeps its activists at their task. It is not always easy to reconcile these faces – at times the ideologist may be confronted by a real dilemma. This was the case in the Labour Party in 1959. In effect, Gaitskell and his followers have tackled the dilemma by pretending that the second horn (the need to bind the organisation together) does not exist.

That the founders of the Labour Party were well aware of the need for solidarity is not surprising. The history of the British Labour movement from the late nineteenth century had shown how division over doctrine could ruin a party. The Social Democratic Federation (as was) had suffered schism, and schism rendered it ineffective. The Independent Labour Party scarcely did better. Indeed, its ability in 1900 to guide the Trades Union Congress to set up the Labour Representation Committee was a small wonder given the ILP's reduced membership.[11] Well did John Wheatley observe in 1925 :

> Looking back over the history of the early days of the Movement it would appear that most of the difficulties arose from too much theorizing and too little actual contact with working class problems.[12]

This is a lesson which had, on the whole, been well learned. Organisations within the party which have a strong doctrinal tendency have repeatedly been made unwelcome. The SDF left of its own accord almost at the beginning. The Communist Party – its heir – has never been allowed back and much effort has been expended in keeping it out. The ILP left having made its all too cogent criticism of the 1929–31 government.[13] Mosley was given no hearing once he proved faintly disloyal. The Socialist League was crushed. Even Nye Bevan and Stafford Cripps could be cold-shouldered when doctrine proved more important to them than loyalty.

All parties, all voluntary organisations, face this problem whether they are working class or not. The organisation needs to hold together. It needs an ideological glue. The Labour Party needs, however, to be particularly careful about not losing members because of the way it is organised. Most of its members are affiliated to it as members of trade unions. These affiliated unions pay dues in a block grant to the party. In 1976 there were fifty-nine unions affiliated to the party and paying the political levy – they paid this levy to the Labour Party on behalf of 5,800,069 members. The number of people who are involved in the decision to affiliate or withdraw from the party is, in the case of each union, very much smaller than the number of members of those unions. I do not suggest the unions are undemocratic. It is simply the case that like all large organisations they are actually run by the small groups of people who work hardest to run them. If any one of these small groups decided to leave the Labour Party and join, say, the Communist Party, Labour could as a result lose a large number of members and a lot of money as well. Its position is thus more precarious than it would be if all members were individual members.

This peculiar method of organisation puts Labour, as a political party in search of voters, in a potentially difficult position. Clause 4 is important to its activists, particularly those in the trade unions; therefore, it must remain where it is. The difficulty becomes actual when such central articles in the activists' faith lose general popularity. The party is then in the position of having to keep ideologically opposed groups of supporters together. Its reaction to this difficulty is, not surprisingly, to fudge the issue. It pursues both groups on the basis of ill-defined feelings of identification like being 'working class'.

To complain that the terms 'working class' and 'class solidarity' are vague or unscientific is simply beside the point. The organisational problem is to hang together, not to clarify the concepts. The question is, where did the idea of class solidarity – which, for all its present popularity and vagueness, is an idea which has had to be learned and now has to be taught – come from? What is the source of this organisational glue? It arises out of a shared past, from a series of folk-memories or shared expression of exploitation, common struggle and gradually increasing power.

<h2 style="text-align:center">III</h2>

In saying that it comes from a past, I use that term deliberately as J. H. Plumb uses it when he distinguishes between 'a past' and 'history'. Plumb's distinction is found in his delightful book *The Death of the Past*.[14] The very paradox of the title points to his unusual use of 'past'. In the ordinary sense in which time passes as a kind of arrow from what is now past to the present on to an unknown future, there can be no sense in which the past is dead. It is merely inert, used-up time which may be remembered or not, or have a history written about it, but most likely not.

What Plumb has in mind, however, is not an abstract bit of used-up time; not 'the past' but 'a past'. He has in mind the way in which collections of half-remembered, often repeated and occasionally embellished tales of a specific past of a specific people – say, the Spartans with their Serpents' Teeth, or the Romans with their Romulus, or the Jews with their march in the wilderness – serve to bind that specific group of people together. A past, in this sense, is a force making for group identity. This past defines 'us'. 'We' are those who have 'suffered under Pharaoh'. . . . In other words, for a people who have a past, part of what they are is their past. In this sense a past is very much alive. It lives in that group whom it identifies, and who keep it alive by repeating it and by reminding each generation of children that 'we' served under Pharaoh. These repetitions serve to perpetuate the group as each generation comes to see itself as those who served under Pharaoh. The group is perpetuated with each generation because each member of each new generation thinks himself a member of the group in so far as he has accepted the events of the past as part of his past. This education is one of the main points of the annual cycle of group holidays. In the course of each whole year salient events from the past are recalled – the Battle of the Boyne refought, the march through the wilderness relived. In such manner a past can be kept alive as long as it is believed. There is nothing about the movement of clocks which diminishes it.

Plumb distinguishes between that sense of a past and history. The point about a past is its vivacity; the point about history is its veracity. History – Plumb here refers to the precise, careful, objective study of times past – kills each past by making it incredible. A past cannot live when it is shown to be not only inaccurate but also not very different from other people's pasts. History dissolves the special provenance of each past. A historical understanding of what has happened is, to develop Plumb's point, very different from a folk-memory. The difference is more than a simple matter of accuracy. The folk-memory's appreciation of times past allows for no development in time. The events of the past are frozen in the memory. For a Jew to associate with the builders of the pyramids, or a worker with the Tolpuddle Martyrs, he has to invoke a timeless category, 'the Jew' or 'the worker'. It is as if Arthur Goldberg were to walk straight from the United States Supreme Court, judicial gowns still flowing, on to the Egyptian desert to move stones for the Pharaoh. In such a memory, not even the ordering of events one before another in chronological sequence has any meaning.[15] There is just the eternal figure 'the Jew', 'the Ulsterman', 'the black', 'the woman', 'the worker', 'the Scot' who suffers oppression. The gap between this kind of appreciation and a historical understanding is not bridged by facts, no matter how numerous; 'history' requires a Parmenidean sense of time's power to dissolve all supposed eternals in its flow. Plumb takes the triumph of the academic study, history, to be complete. An army of industrious fact-mongers has slowly but finally discovered so many records of various pasts that no one past can be believed. Hence his talk of the death of the past. In that last judgement, at least, I must differ from him.

As a general point, people whose identity is threatened by history-books do not cease believing as a result of what has been written. People are fully capable of isolating history and not taking it seriously.

Anthropologists like F. G. Bailey, Pierre Bourdieu and E. E. Evans-Pritchard, and sociologists like W. Moore have located such groups of people.[16] I can cite two contemporary British groups who have a living past in Plumb's sense: Ulstermen and the more class-conscious parts of the British working class. Many of the biographies of working men's – and womens' – lives bear witness to this truth. Jennie Lee's autobiography *This Great Journey* provides a moving example of witness. In that book it is sometimes difficult to tell the difference between the struggle of the person and the class, so closely does the author identify herself with her people. An extended quotation will make the point. She is writing about the time when she and Aneurin Bevan had returned home from Spain in 1938, and were deeply depressed by what they had seen and by the recognition that their Labour Party was doing nothing about it:

> Why was Aneurin so often sad now? Why did my father sit by the fire, gently cynical about the whole socialist movement that had once been for him ground so sacred that he taught us to tread reverently whenever we approached it? . . . Where was all the vigour, the belligerency, the robust certainties that had characterised the Labour movement as I remembered it in my teens and early twenties? . . . I decided I would begin my quest by strolling through the town, talking less and listening more. . . . I wanted to know what people were thinking about some of the decisions the Labour Party conference had just reached. . . . All these men had lived through phases of intense social and political concern. More than once they had thought that Jerusalem was just around the corner. . . . There had never been a time when they had not rebelled against the raw, racking poverty and labour of a miner's life.
> The struggle to build a union, a Co-operative movement, a socialist party; the eager reading of books and pamphlets and the weekly socialist press. . . . We talked until the darkness closed round the fireside and the curtains had to be drawn. . . . But there was no electric light in the Lochgelly, our minds had travelled to. . . . 'Don't lose heart lass. Don't lose heart. If you can spin it out, we will beat them yet.' . . . She was telling us about 1870 and '71. The Fife miners are fighting for the eight hours' working-day. I forget the present. I have gone back more than sixty years. I am a collier hewing coal. . . . I pledged myself to my workmates. None of us to work a minute longer than eight hours. . . . I must stand true. . . . But patience, 'thole a bit longer, and we will win yet! Alexander MacDonald said we could. He had a grand turnout to his meeting on the Birnae Braes. . . . And what can a man do? The Company has the pull. It has the money and the power. There is only one thing we have; just one weapon in our hands. We can hold together,

keep our plighted word, not give in, stick whatever suffering may be entailed until the company learns. . . . And so racked with anger, sorrow and labour, the miners of Fife in 1870. . . . The years pass. It is 1894. I am my grandfather sitting by the roadside wondering where next I can turn. I have been a ringleader in a recent strike. . . . 1897 – the coal company thinks it can dictate even who my doctor is to be. I won't submit. . . . 1898 – I have been elected to the Lochgelly Town Council. . . . For several years I had been living with a great fear; the fear that my grandfather's movement was a doomed thing. . . . Not because it had championed the cause of the poor too strenuously, but because, again and again, since 1926, when it ought to have stood its ground, it had found plausible reasons for running away.[17]

This truly is a living past which serves to comfort the members of the group when they are dispirited and guide them in their action.

It is interesting that Norman Dennis observed much the same idiom and same creative use of the past amongst the miners of a Yorkshire mining village in his study *Coal Is Our Life*.[18] People brought up in such traditions, such as Jennie Lee and Aneurin Bevan, often feel a very strong sense of obligation to those who have struggled before them. Of course, not all miners were as radical as those in Fife; the Nottinghamshire and Derbyshire miners were much more respectable than their Scottish brothers and supported the Liberals well into this century – and, in any case, miners are special. There can be no doubt that the isolated existence of mining villages, away from the large urban centres, enables them to protect and cherish their special past in a way which is not possible for other groups of workers. For other workers the sense of a shared past is perhaps not so vivid, but it exists and serves the same functions as in the miners' case. Thus, I think Plumb's almost eighteenth-century optimism about the triumph of history is unjustified. Just to complicate the picture a bit, it is obvious that it is possible to create or re-create a past which has never existed or which has ceased to exist. A past, in this sense, may be a myth. Since such pasts are impervious to history, few are without some mythical elements. Many national histories have been more or less deliberately so created. Scottish national history is being recreated at this very moment.

The fact that Plumb is a distinguished historian of the eighteenth century is interesting in itself, for the move from the perception of 'pasts' to 'history' was part of a larger change of consciousness of time which was going on in eighteenth-century England. Previously there had been a consciousness of change and a series of natural cycles – the cycle of day and night, of the seasons, of the years, of life and death – now there developed a concept of 'time' as a commodity which would be very precisely measured, used and spent. This was a movement, as the anthropological literature describes it, from cyclical time to clock-time.[19]

Clock-time, which is necessary to any (capitalist or other) industrial society, admits of three dimensions: past, present and future. Though each particular moment is equal in that it is successively part of the future, this present, and the past, its value alters radically as it moves through this sequence. Past time is used up and of no value; present time is valuable but fleeting; future time or, rather, the present preparation or planning for future time is of supreme importance. By planning now for future moments we can make the best possible use of them when they arrive. Planning is the ordering of priorities which makes it possible for us to change the character of our time.

Thus, we see that a world which lives by clock-time is going to be one – as, indeed, ours is – which puts immense value on the future. Clock-time also provides us with the conceptual link between planning and the future. Cyclical time, on the contrary, values the past. In a society which lives by cyclical time an elderly person is valued for his experience. He has been through all this before. Those whom we call 'the elderly' and imply by this people who no longer have useful time at their command – used-up people – they call 'the venerable'. Time lived serves in that world to establish a social hierarchy; the older a man is, the more experience he has and hence the wiser he becomes.

When clock-time replaced cyclical time the past lost its standing and the future gained. When the social democrats urge that Labour is a party of the future, what they say is in harmony with the dominant time-perspective of our age. From this perspective being 'modern', 'up-to-date', '*au fait*', is praised and dwelling on, or living in, the past, condemned. Against it I think I need simply say that clock-time provides an inadequate understanding of how time is actually experienced.

A sense of a common past binds people together. Such a shared past is also the 'organisational glue' of the Labour movement and of the party. The strength of the glue is perhaps strongest where it is most needed: amongst the politically sensitive activists. Amongst the electorate it has been strong enough. Butler and Stokes quote a Stirling worker's wife explaining her support for Labour by saying, 'I always vote for them, it's a working man's place to vote Labour'. They report that their research 'makes it clear how very much more salient to the working class are the ideas of class interest and class conflict. Seven in eight of our working-class Labour supporters gave evidence of seeing politics as the representation of class interest, and almost half regarded such interests as opposed.'[20] The various factors which previously divided a class, such as craft, locality and religion, have increasingly been put aside and overcome as the members of a class have realised that they were being treated as just so many interchangeable workers.[21] The strongest memories which serve to build this sense of identity are those in which the class is rejected.

The folk-memories which have gone into the making of the British working class – the making of which is by no means complete – are of immense value to the Labour Party because, since 1900, the party has so often been associated, though perhaps not as closely as it might like to believe, with the class. Michael Foot, speaking as Bevan's biographer, notes that for Bevan, rebel that he occasionally was:

> . . . the Labour Party was his life. . . . The deed required an instrument and in Britain that instrument was the Labour Party. Moreover, this instrument had a history, interwoven with the struggles and fears and triumphs of his own people and the land of his fathers. Touched by his romantic wand, the political party, for all its intrigues and inadequacies, could be transformed into a shining crusade.[22]

The party has all along gained support as it identified itself with this crusade. One can instance here the anti-trade union Acts and judicial decisions at the turn of the century – most especially Taff Vale, which drove many into the Labour Representation Committee. After Taff Vale the party gained support as it was seen that all would be lost without a working-class party. There is also the memory of the rejection and betrayal of Labour's leaders by Lloyd George in the First World War, which taught Labour that it could not depend on pacts with bourgeois parties. Most of all, there is the memory of the long, intense and bitter depression – epitomised by the failure of the General Strike – and the hateful refusal of the Tory leadership to do anything about unemployment.[23]

All of these memories of the rejection of the movement and its leadership, or of working people, redound to the advantage of Labour now. This advantage, if one listens to the talk amongst party workers in the committee-rooms, is not lessened by certain historical awkwardnesses such as Snowden's meanness as Chancellor or MacDonald's tepidness during the General Strike. But, then, one is talking about 'a past' and not writing 'history'; this only makes it more difficult and foolish to raise awkward questions in the wrong places.

Rejection is not the only politically valuable memory. Labour's victories – most especially the creation of the national health service, but also the effectiveness of Ernie Bevin and Clem Attlee in the War Cabinet and their later success as Foreign Secretary and Prime Minister respectively, the nationalisation of the mines and the railways, the ending of the Poor Law – all are of some help. Labour's achievements, though hardly on the lips of every voter, are the things Labour activists will spontaneously mention with pride and which certainly serve to impel them to their necessary humdrum tasks. As in rejection, so in victory, what matters is the memory, not the fact. The Ulster example is again illuminating; it seems not to matter amongst Orangemen that the Pope backed their Protestant hero 'King Billy' at the Boyne against King James. The point, in each case, is that the memory of victory past reinforces the strength of group loyalty and identity.

IV

But victory has its price in these matters. If Labour's legislative victories are frequent enough, and if the Tories have the sense not to challenge them once they are achieved; if, even more, the leadership of the Tory Party has the sense to woo and incorporate the trade union leaders into its establishment and, however temporarily, abandon its primary job; then Labour's separate identity is threatened. Nationalisation of medical care, for example, or the imposition of a wealth tax, may be strongly resisted by the property party when Labour is out of power. They will even be resisted when Labour is in power but does not act because of, say, a currency crisis. During a period of challenge by the Labour Party and resistance by the Conservatives, it is easy enough to see where Labour stands. Immediately it succeeds in reform the situation loses its clarity. The Conservative governments of 1951–64 did not make an assault of principle against the health service – they may have weakened it by degrees, but that is another problem – and, once they were seen to operate the health service, the benefit derived from it was no longer the exclusive political property of the Labour Party. Thus, memory of victory is dulled. Those annual ceremonies in which the movement relives its memories – May Day Rallies, Miners' Galas, Burns' Suppers and the like – are not sufficient in themselves and they would lose their charm unless the stock of memories were replenished. The home, too, must play an important part, for it is here that so many of us learn to identify with one or other party. Sometimes the Conservative Party is foolish enough to provide Labour with an opportunity to rebuild its position. The passing of the Industrial Relations Act by the Conservative administration led by Mr Heath – and especially the way that government failed to consult the unions beforehand – was such an example, but such opportunities can scarcely be expected often. Labour was built as an opposition party; the glue which holds it together would melt if it ceased in some sense to remain an opposition party. It has a real stake, then, in remaining out.

Labour's first long period of office, 1940–51, first in coalition and then alone, was followed by a Butskellite Conservative administration. This period posed a threat on precisely these grounds. To be fair to Gaitskell, his 1959 speech was an attempt to force this danger to the party's attention. He saw Clause 4 as a tie to the past which as such was of no use. My objection to this is twofold. First, in arguing for the deletion of Clause 4, on the grounds that it no longer led to intelligent policy,* Gaitskell was overlooking the immense symbolic value which a continuous tradition of opposition to capitalism had for Labour. He was forgetting the strength of the ethos of the party – and it was ultimately for this reason that his proposal was dropped.

Secondly, Clause 4, so fundamentally associated with the Labour Party, was more than a sentimental symbol. As Arthur Henderson realised when it was adopted, it puts a principle between Labour and the Tories. As long as Labour retains Clause 4, the Tories can never assimilate all of Labour's achievements or demands. The national health service can be assimilated by a Conservative government, and so, too, in prosperous days can strong trade unions, but 'the common ownership of the means of production, distribution and exchange' cannot. Thus, Clause 4's continuance as the sole statement of principle in Labour's constitution holds Labour true to its past, true to what its originators wanted it to be: *for* labour and *against* capital. The special position of Clause 4 is that it is a statement of principle which has policy implications and yet one which ensures that the party remains true to its ethos.

To judge by the events sparked by the electoral defeat of 1959 we may suggest that this special position is occasionally less impressive to the National Executive Committee and the Cabinet than to annual conference and the trade unions. The NEC and Cabinet responded more to the demands of electoral politics. For example, they wanted to go to the electorate in 1945 without a specific commitment to take over anything. The Executive had lost its way. The conference, led by the Transport and General Workers' Union, remembered, as they would have it, what they were there for. But even within conference the force of feeling is not constant. When the blood is up – in 1918, 1945 and 1973 – there is more interest in socialism (as Clause 4 is sometimes called) than at other times. In fact Gaitskell and his colleagues succeeded in raising interest in Clause 4 at a time when it was not very high by threatening to remove it. The crucial factor, as always, is what key unions think. The conference is usually most unwilling to propose a change unless the unions whose interests are most directly involved are prepared to move.

---

*The assumption is often made that Clause 4 leads necessarily to the Morrisonian Public Corporation. This is not so. It is consistent with any form of social control.

V

Since Labour's ethos emanates from a specific past one may ask what the implications of this tie are for the party. I have already alluded to the first: Labour cannot be *simpliciter* a party of the future. Such a possibility may be available to a radical social democratic party. It is not possible for the historic Labour Party. The attempt by Crosland in his *The Future of Socialism* (happy title) (1956) to condemn Labour's tendency to cling to the principles of its past is futile.[24] Any attempt to redefine goals for future action must always be seen to be strictly consonant with its past.

A second implication is that Labour's support can be eroded by a general change of consciousness.[25] If the ties of class-consciousness are weakened, then Labour is threatened. Similarly, if Labour comes to be seen as an increasingly middle-class organisation, it could lose its support even if its former supporters remained class-conscious. Crosland and Gaitskell saw the first of these threats without recognising the second. Class-consciousness, as a historical fact, is obviously endangered by changes external to it. Gaitskell saw prosperity as one such threat. Nationalism is another – one whose power is more real in the 1970s than could have been foreseen in the late 1950s. As Scottish and Welsh working people come to identify themselves as Scots or Welshmen first and workers second, Labour loses their support to the nationalist parties. As this happens, one witnesses an exchange of one past for another as the new choice comes to appear more vivid. If in future general elections Labour loses parliamentary seats as a result, it will be paying a high price for the loss of class-identity.

It is, I think, a matter of historical fact that the annual cycle of rituals in which Labour celebrates and relives its past is losing popularity.[26] May Day rallies in particular attract fewer people each year. There seems to be a general lack of enthusiasm for such rituals, even by people who are prepared to work very hard during an election campaign. The threat to unity from this tepidness is too real to need emphasis. Reasons for it are varied: readily available alternative forms of entertainment, the abrupt destruction of familiar neighbourhoods and ties through 'urban renewal', the failure of local and national leadership to temper the old ceremonies with popular new techniques, even occasionally a willingness to take not only Labour's voters but also the whole system for granted – all these contrive to weaken the ties of memory on which so much depends.

Thirdly, and most interestingly of all, Labour's tie to its own past affects its ideas about change. 'What is to be done?' One has to begin here by stating the obvious: Labour is not an extremist party. Neither its trade union leaders nor its middle-class intellectuals are extremists. Labour is more closely tied to its trade unionists than any other major party in any major country. They set the tone of its thought. The experience of trade unionists does not lend itself to extreme demands. The business of a union is to get the best possible arrangement for its members. This raises shrewd and sagacious men to the fore, men who are tough negotiators. It makes leaders of men who know how to make demands and take risks, but also men who can judge what capital can pay. This is an attitude of mind which says, 'We will make these levers work for us'.[27] It is an attitude which knows the power of loyalty and makes for caution.

It is a caution which values tried practices and self-reliance. Hence its elephantine progress, so infuriating to Continental socialists. Hence, too, its willingness to support a parliamentary rather than a revolutionary political party. The British trade union movement lacks the experience (since 1868, and Ulster excluded) of successful revolutionary activity. In its ventures into revolution – Glasgow in 1919, the General Strikes of 1926 and 1972 – it has been either out-manoeuvred or divided (or both) or reduced to farce. Such experience is not the stuff of dreams. British trade unions have an experience of success with overtime bans, 'go-slows', overmanning, and supporting the Labour Party. That is to say, their success has been at undermining the system, sabotaging its intentions and using its structure against its rulers and owners.

With this kind of incrementalist project, Labour attracts to it those planners from amongst the country's white-collar workers who are by disposition or profession inclined to a similar view. Those, on the other hand, who cannot accept such slow-paced change are simply attracted to other parties. In contrast to some prominent Continental socialist parties, the Austrian for instance, the pace of the Labour Party is set by its unions. Just how the intellectuals and the political leadership deal with this pace is the stuff of Labour's history. In a party whose central myth is its democracy, and whose membership is made up overwhelmingly of people who are affiliated to it as trade unionists, the unions dominate. Significantly, union support for Gaitskell helped him become leader, and union opposition to his position on Clause 4 made it impossible for him to erase it.

It is perhaps too easy to argue from this that Labour is a backward-looking party. To the extent that it is a backward-looking party – and the charge cannot be completely denied – this is a corruption. A party with a strong sense of its own tradition is not necessarily backward-looking. Whether it is, or not, depends first of all on the positive content of its tradition. A party formed to force a return to some real or imagined past state of affairs, such as national independence and glory, or a party which cannot raise its sights above some past victory or victories, such as 1776 or 1789 or 1918, is backward-looking.[28] But Labour was formed to defend the working class ultimately by ending capitalism, and while it can legitimately claim some success at this there is no real doubt that there is still work to do.

Labour's ideology is not merely backward-looking, for all the strength of its past, because that past, the experience of exploitation and the gradual overcoming of it, implicitly embodies the socialist project. The only place where this is made explicit is in Clause 4, and in the various unions' constitutions which embody a similar statement. The symbolic importance which attaches to this slender clause derives from the fact that this is the only place where the constitution actually says that the Labour Party is dedicated to a complete takeover of power by the working class. The point about socialism is not efficiency, nor the equality of income which might result from its realisation, but the fact that it represents the replacement of one order by another, the rule of the capitalists by that of the workers. This project is at once cautiously forward-looking and rooted in a particular past.

It is forward-looking in that it is a promise, a will to action, and an agreed method of progress. It is not definite or precise. It leaves some of the central questions like the method of social control or the position of the workers open. It is in these indefinite areas where doctrinaires and planners have some scope for their operations – but little more than that. On the method of reaching the goal there is much more agreement. Parliamentary democracy and (preferably legal) trade union pressure will be used to end capitalism. Radical whiggery, one could call this; and, if there is a paradox in moving to a revolution by the use of conventional means, so be it.

But this is not a forward-looking plan which ignores the past. On the contrary, the socialist project is refreshed, and the will to achieve it is rekindled, by recalling how far one has come already and how one has done it. The past can sustain the project. The job for the ideologist and the leaders is to make tactical plans which harmonise with it. Whether this can be done for the Conservative Party or not is a question which, I think, must be left to Conservatives. Certainly, Jennie Lee doubted it. Reflecting on Churchill's performances in the House of Commons during the Second World War, she thought:

> I tried to understand what was in his mind. How did he see the future? Could he be brought to realise that the British Empire in the form he had known it, loved it, approved of it, had come to an end? That the great imperial dream his ancestors had begun for him would now have to give ground to the still greater dream my forebears had begun for me? The Prime Minister was as primitive in his loyalties as I was in mine. He was an ancestor worshipper.

So was I. He believed in the future of his countrymen. So did I.
But it was different ancestors we worshipped and different futures
we believed in.[29]

NOTES

1   Viscount Hailsham, *The Conservative Case* (London, 1959), pp. 12–13.
     See also Lord Hugh Cecil, *Conservatism* (London, 1912), especially ch.
     1 and 2; Lord Blake, *The Conservative Party from Peel to Churchill*
     (London, 1970), the introduction.
2   Winter, J. M., *Socialism and the Challenge of War: Ideas and Politics
     1912–1918* (London, 1974), chs 8 and 9.
3   Wilson, Harold, 'Parliamentary report', *Labour Party Annual Conference
     Report 1966*, p. 169.
4   These remarks are suggested by Albert Camus, who, in *The Rebel*,
     defends such rebellion. Camus seems to me mistaken in his historical
     judgements, but a thinker whose writing invariably opens up new ideas.
     What I am saying here actually follows closely some of the occasional
     remarks Michels tosses off in his *Political Parties*; see the New York
     edition of 1915, reprinted in 1959, pp. 238–9.
5   Winter, *Socialism and the Challenge of War*, p. 259.
6   Tawney, R. H., 'The choice before the Labour Party', *Political
     Quarterly*, 1932, in Robson, W. A., *Political Quarterly in the Thirties*
     (London, 1971), p. 96.
7   Harrison, R., 'Labour government: then and now', *Political Quarterly*,
     vol. 41, no. 1, January–March 1973, pp. 71–2, 78. For an earlier
     instance of the same argument, see Thompson, E. P., 'Homage to Tom
     McQuire', in Briggs, A., and Savile, J. (eds), *Essays in Labour History*
     (London, 1967), pp. 312–13.
8   Mackintosh, J. P., 'Socialism or social democracy: the choice for the
     Labour Party', *Political Quarterly*, vol. 43, no. 4, 1972, pp. 473–4.
9   Gaitskell, H., in *Report of the 58th Annual Conference of the Labour
     Party 1959*, p. 109.
10   Wedgwood Benn, A., in *Report of the 58th Annual Conference of the
     Labour Party 1959*, p. 116.
11   The ILP was down to a quarter of its previous peak membership and
     nearly bankrupt. See Bealey, F., and Pelling, H., *Labour and Politics
     1900–1906* (London, 1958), p. 160.
12   Wheatley, J., 'Why a Labour Party?' in Tracey, H., *The Book of the
     Labour Party*, Vol. 1 (London, 1925), p. 44. Wheatley's views were
     echoed repeatedly at annual conferences.
13   See Middlemas, R. K., *The Clydesiders: A Left Wing Struggle for
     Parliamentary Power* (London, 1965); compare Skidelsky, R., *Politicians
     and the Slump: The Labour Government of 1929–31* (London, 1967),
     who gives all the credit for the new ideas to the Liberals.
14   Plumb, J. H., *The Death of the Past* (Harmondsworth, 1973).
15   Rosenzeig, F., *The Star of Redemption* (London, 1971), pp. 337–8.
16   See Bailey, F. G., 'The peasant view of the bad life', in Shanin, T.,
     Peasants and Peasant Societies (Harmondsworth, 1971), pp. 299–321.
     Bourdieu, P., 'The attitude of the Algerian peasant towards time', in
     Pitt-Rivers, J. (ed.), *Mediterranean Countrymen* (Paris, 1963); Evans-
     Pritchard, E. E., 'Time in not a continuum', in Douglas, M., *Rules and
     Meanings: The Anthropology of Everyday Knowledge* (Harmondsworth,
     1973), pp. 75–81; Moore, W., *Man, Time and Society* (London, 1963).

17 Lee, J., *This Great Journey* (London, 1963), pp. 169–75.
18 Dennis, N., *et al.*, *Coal is Our Life* (London, 1956), p. 83.
19 ibid., pp. 130–1; see interesting contrast with middle-class professionals, p. 139.
20 Butler, D., and Stokes, D., *Political Change in Britain: Forces Shaping Electoral Choice* (Harmondsworth, 1971), p. 121.
21 Thompson, E. P., *The Making of the English Working Class* (London, 1963).
22 Foot, M., *Aneurin Bevin: A Biography 1945–60* (London, 1973), p. 49.
23 See Gorman, J., *Banner Bright: An Illustrated History of the Banners of the British Trade Union Movement* (London, 1973).
24 Crosland, C. A. R., *The Future of Socialism* (London, 1963; 1st edn, 1956). See pp. 43–5.
25 To my knowledge Marx never addressed himself to this possibility, but certainly the drift of his theory of historical materialism is that such retrogression was not possible. The Marxist answer, however, is clear enough: 'class consciousness has never been created in the full sense in Britain'. Instead one has 'trade union consciousness'. I reject this – but this is not the place to develop the argument.
26 See Hindess, B., *The Decline of Working-Class Politics* (London, 1971), where the decline is taken too far. The generalisation in this book is from Liverpool experience (in any case an untypical city) over a short historical period.
27 See Bullock, A., *The Life and Times of Ernest Bevin* Vol. 1 (London, 1960). Bevin, who was one of the shrewdest of them all, once attributed this kind of conservatism to the defensive outlook of his members: 'The most conservative man in the world is the British trade unionist when you want to change him. You can make a great speech on unity, but when you are finished he will say, "What about the funeral benefits?"' (p. 383).
28 Nairn, T., 'Scotland: anomaly in Europe', *New Left Review*, no. 33, January–March 1974, pp. 57–82.
29 Lee, *This Great Journey*, p. 223.

3
Labour's Doctrines: Is Socialism about Equality?

I

Since the demise of the Attlee government – at any rate, since its loss of heart in the winter of 1947–8 – there has been a series of moves away from the doctrinal positions then held by the left of the party. I think we can distinguish four different positions which have been taken up.

The fatherest-left position, which has considerable support amongst constituency activists, holds that socialism is about nationalisation. Its proponents want – and expect – Labour to use government to make wholesale takeovers of privately owned industries. This view was common until 1951. No organised body of parliamentary opinion now supports it, though election manifestos do occasionally allude to it. The 1974 manifesto, for instance, promised 'a fundamental and irreversible shift in the balance of wealth and power in favour of working people and their families'.

The second position, now occupied by much of the Tribune Group, is that first staked out by Herbert Morrison in 1950–1. Originally known as 'consolidationism', this position urges the careful protection of gains already made with only limited further takeovers. Consolidationism was about the more efficient operation of already publicly owned firms. It became a credible political position when union leaders and cabinet members had sated their original appetites.

Gradually this position ceased to be the specific property of Herbert Morrison and his friends and was developed to include the idea that the already nationalised firms should now be socialised; that is, they should be run more by their workers and in the interests of their consumers, and less by remote officials. Consolidationism is an honourable fulfilment of Clause 4. It was this position which the Gaitskellites, most notably C. A. R. Crosland, sought to revise.

The third position is that staked out by Crosland and known

variously as revisionism, social democracy and democratic socialism. It is about men as citizens and consumers, not as workers. It calls for large increases in public expenditure to pay for the new improved services needed to ameliorate inequalities. When first enunciated by Crosland, revisionism was an attempt to move Labour away from the old left socialist doctrines; these doctrines were conflated by the revisionists when they attacked them.

The fourth position has only recently begun to be discernible. It is the position taken up by the Labour government elected in 1974 and is perhaps best described as corporate socialism. According to this view socialism cannot be understood as any particular policy or doctrine but, rather, as whatever policies the TUC leadership and a Labour Cabinet agree are in the national interest at the moment. This new position, which seems to have become the official operating principle of the party, and which was originally embodied in the 'social contract', does not currently embrace either a large measure of nationalisation or even a defence of the current level of public expenditure. It is a purely procedural notion and devoid of specific content. It is the product, in part, of a severe depression; economic depression weakens the bargaining power of the unions and makes them more pliable. It is also the product of the extreme political ineptitude within the Conservative Party, which has driven the TUC leaders into the embrace of the Labour Party's leaders despite the party's own attack on the unions in the late 1960s.

Corporate socialism, if it ever becomes a fully elaborated doctrine, will be a form of extreme pragmatism. It has no goal, but possesses an astute and sensitive awareness of what it wants to protect: the economic standards of employed working-class men. It is really very similar to the position taken up by the party leadership before 1914. I find it difficult to believe that it can avoid the sorts of difficulties which beset that early 'pre-socialist' leadership. Not knowing where it wants to go, it will end in confusion. This emerging doctrine has claim to the title 'socialist' only by courtesy of birth: it carries the surname of its father. It is 'corporate' in that it takes its cues from agreements between two of the great British corporations: the General Council of the TUC and the Labour leadership.

Of course, no ideology is an entirely coherent body of ideas, and many ideologists seem to enjoy fighting their fellow-believers at least as much as the enemy outside. Self-confessed anti-ideologists find this fighting distasteful and a sign of an imminent *auto-da-fé* of the ideology.[1] Theirs is a superficial view. Ideological disputes over the meaning of the central notions of the ideology are not to be despised, or even seen as a sign of weakness. People usually fight hardest over ground which is important to them; and, on the other hand, concede agreement on things which are less important to them. No one would take the annual battles within the Cabinet for increased allocations as a sign that money was disreputable or unsound. Similarly, the disputes within an ideology over its meaning are a sign of the vitality of the participants and the importance to them of the ground they dispute.

We can, I think, gain some insight into these disputes within the Labour Party by examining the challenge made by the egalitarians to the older positions. So in this chapter I will examine the intellectual and political bases of the egalitarian doctrine. The most cogent and often-cited statement of it is found in the writings of C. A. R. Crosland.

Crosland began his final book, *Socialism Now*, with the following self-confident assertion:

There is, at least, no need for revisionists to revise our definition of socialism. Socialism in our view, was basically about equality. By equality, we meant more than a meritacratic society of equal opportunities in which the greatest rewards went to those with the most fortunate genetic endowment and family background. . . . We also meant more than a simple (not that it proved simple in practice) redistribution of income. We wanted a wider social equality embracing also the distribution of property, the educational system, social-class relationships, power and privilege in industry – indeed all that was enshrined in the age-old socialist dream of a more 'classless society'.[2]

Crosland there records, or claims, a victory for the revisionist definition of socialism – socialism was about equality. This is a definition for which he had been trying to win acceptance since the publication of his first book, *The Future of Socialism* (1956). The earlier book was the central text of the revisionist or, as it was sometimes called, social democratic school, which included Douglas Jay, Hugh Gaitskell, Roy Jenkins and J. P. Mackintosh among others.[3]

In contrast to Crosland an important tradition of usage on the left of the Labour Party closely associates socialism with nationalisation. Socialism, in this tradition, is first of all about the ownership of the means of production, not about the principles of distribution of the things produced.[4] Socialism is here seen as the replacement of a system in which the means of production are privately owned, and used to produce profit, by one in which the tools of production are publicly owned. The large public corporation – the Gas Council, the National Coal Board, British Railways, the Electricity Generating Board – was the Labour Party's chosen form of public control. The process of replacement of private by public control by means of a parliamentary Bill which fixed compensation for the assets taken over was known as nationalisation.*

The social democrats' belief that socialism was about equality was a direct challenge to this 'production socialism' position. With some pardonable licence Crosland associated the 'production socialist' position with Marx. Revisionism, as he put it in 1974, maintained, contrary to the traditional Marxist doctrine, that the ownership of the means of production was no longer the key factor which imparted to a society its essential character'.[5] The truth is that the revisionists were not greatly interested in the production of wealth. Or, rather, they were uninterested in how it was produced because they believed that, no matter how it was produced, the government could manage the economy to produce a gradually increasing amount of wealth. The real task in their view, then, was to see to its equitable distribution.

The revisionist thesis was underwritten by the belief that Labour was being hampered at elections by its commitment to further nationalisation; by Clause 4 of its constitution. The major wave of revisionist thinking came in the wake of the electoral retreats of 1950, 1951 and 1955. The strongest confirmation of this belief was found in a survey commissioned from Mark Abrams and published in *Socialist Commentary* (and subsequently in book form as *Must Labour Lose?* by Abrams, Rose and Rita Hinden).[6] Abrams had depressing news for Labour: only 2 per cent of the survey's sample looked forward to future nationalisation under a future Labour government; 33 per cent were seriously frightened by the prospect;[7] young people (under-25s) were farther to the right than their elders;[8] young people did not like Labour's cloth-cap image – they identified themselves mainly with middle-class people, forward looking people, office workers, and ambitious people;[9] 'there is among young people today a complex of barely conscious Conservative sympathies which have still not yet fully expressed themselves in overt party affiliations';[10] 'it is immediately apparent that the Labour Party's traditional source of support in the environment, in individual values, and in Party loyalties have been weakening';[11] 'Labour is thought of as a predominantly class party and that class which it represents is objectively and subjectively on the wane';[12] the Labour leader, Hugh Gaitskell, was less respected than the Tory leader, Harold Macmillan;[13] and, just in case Labour had any hope left, the authors observed, 'It would take an unusually large swing in votes to Labour, about 4%, to turn out the Conservative government at the next election. The largest swing at a post-war election, 3·1% came in 1950, and it was to the Conservatives'.[14]

*Names count for a lot here. 'Nationalisation' was applied to central government takeovers of some local government enterprises – gas boards for example – but not others – hospitals most noticeably. To protect doctors' *amour-propre*?

From that depressing hail of blows it was possible to draw any of several lessons. The Bevanites and R. H. S. Crossman, in particular, took these poll results to show that socialists should turn their backs on the electorate and that, in effect, the electorate was unworthy of socialism. It seemed to them that the party must return to the electoral wilderness to re-educate the people in socialism.[15] The revisionists, on the other hand, even considered changing the name of the party to erase the cloth-cap image. They decided to try to turn the party away from a concern with the ownership of the means of production and towards social equality. Given a continued commitment to winning elections, this was a reasonable strategy.

The case the revisionists put for softening Labour's attachment to Clause 4 had many facets: that the commitment to Clause 4 was of recent origin and not as venerable as that to equality; that even when Labour was committed to Clause 4 it was never more than a commitment to it as a means to an end; that experience showed that two of the more important ends for which public control was urged (that the problems in some industries, coal especially, could not be resolved while so many different private companies were involved; and that efficient national planning required large shares of public ownership) could not be further advanced by more nationalisation; that nationalisation did not lead to a more equitable distribution of wealth, because of the compensation paid; that what mattered in industry was control, not ownership; that nationalised industries were run by bureaucracies not very different in aim, methods or effect from those which ran large firms (and that such bureaucracies were a result of large size and not of ownership); that nationalisation was an old-fashioned remedy; and that, in a political world, it made no sense to be committed to a policy that was so unpopular that commitment to it would ensure that those committed were never elected to carry it – or anything else – out.

All this is to say that the revisionists entered the argument on the level of discussion of major policy. They fully realised that their argument was not being met on that level. They understood that the left clung to Clause 4 for reasons which they had not controverted; but this recognition, far from leading the two sides to forget their differences, just led to mutual contempt. On the revisionists' side the contempt is clear in Crosland's work; Jenkins confined himself to the laconic observation that the revisionists had overestimated the role of reason in human affairs.[16] Haseler, the historian of revisionism, merely notes, sadly, that 'The party was attached to Clause 4 in a sentimental way rather than as a basis for future policy proposals'.[17] The revisionists wanted to orient Labour's policy around the principle of equality. To do this they tried to show that nationalisation was not a coherent principle or a sensible policy and that, in any case, it was not what the voters wanted. The Bevanites clung to Clause 4 partly because it was a totem at the heart of their mythology. For their part they were willing to make Clause 4 an end in itself, because it was what 'their' people (the majority of the constituency parties, for instance) wanted.

II

One problem for the revisionists was that they had not really thought out the question of means and ends. Their equality was hardly in a better position than the Bevanites' Clause 4 to be put forward as an end. There was a muddle about the meaning of 'equality' in the heart of the revisionists' thesis. Tawney, whose work on the subject is better thought out than Crosland's, distinguished carefully between equality before the law and, following from it, political equality (one man, one vote, one value). These two principles had been achieved in stages in Britain by 1928 (when votes for women under 30 were granted). But it is clear that political democracy is a charade without economic and social equality. Economic and social equality were taken to imply, at first, equality of opportunity. Equality of opportunity could only be achieved by a system of careers open to talent and an egalitarian school system. Much work had been done towards these goals in the nineteenth century. Careers, especially careers in the civil service, were open to entry by examination; they were no longer toys of patronage. This was an important step in attacking aristocratic power and in establishing the dominance of the middle class. Patently, however, a completely new school system was required for careers to be open to talented working-class children.

Crosland's *Future of Socialism* pointed out how much had to be done to change the school system to make equality of opportunity a reality for working-class children. His work did much to reawaken the party to the need for further advances on this front. Previously, the party had accepted the major features of the school system enacted by the coalition government and a Conservative minister (R. A. Butler) and, strange though it seems now, turned away from the subject almost entirely. Crosland's achievement in reawakening the party to the task that had to be done is not to be belittled. It is interesting that when Crosland became Minister for Education in the 1966 government he was responsible for encouraging local authorities to establish comprehensive schools. Yet it is far from clear that the introduction of comprehensive school systems has made much impact on social inequality. One reason for this is that many other forces affecting social inequality have been at work; another is that so many other changes were being made to the education system at the same time that it has proved all but impossible to measure the effect of any one of them.[18]

And that is the main charge against equality of opportunity as a policy: it assumes that the rest of society remains constant. It assumes a basically hierarchical society with wide differences of wealth and respect up through which bright working-class lads can climb helped by a comprehensive state-run school system. In this sense equality of opportunity assumes the continuance of an inegalitarian society. In another sense its effect, over time, may be to perpetuate inequalities since it operates to deprive working-class people of their naturally talented leaders as these talented ones climb the success ladder.

For reasons of this kind, equality of opportunity has often been attacked as a hopelessly insufficient basis for socialism. Tawney so attacked it. The early Fabians, on the other hand, embraced equality of opportunity and so, too, in practice, do most East European socialist countries. In these countries, admission to various positions of trust and power depends, much more strikingly than in the West – where parental wealth, personal acumen and experience play a role – upon acquiring educational qualifications. Too easily the enactment of the principle 'from each according to his ability' becomes 'to each according to his ability' and establishes a new kind of rigid hierarchical society.

The interesting or, if one prefers, the depressing thing about the place of the principle of equality of income in British socialism is that it runs directly contrary to some of the most deeply entrenched practices of trade unions. Indeed, it is obvious that any egalitarian principle about the distribution of income conflicts with trade union practice. That practice gives rise to the method of bargaining known as 'free collective bargaining' – which most definitely does not entail an egalitarian approach to distribution. It is the business of trade unions and their officials first to defend and, where possible, to advance the wages of their members. It follows from this that the Labour Party in its present constitution is simply not going to accept equality of income as a principle. Unless it undergoes an internal revolution first, it will simply never dance to that tune. In this, not insignificant, respect the Labour Party is one of the safest bastions of the *status quo*. Both Marxists and revisionists are out of touch if they ignore that fact.

Crosland and the revisionists were, of course, very much concerned to move to a society in which, at very least, inequalities of income were less great than at present. Indeed, one thing which emboldened them to claim that socialism was about equality was their belief that Labour had actually succeeded in 1945–51 in ironing out the worst inequalities of income.

Tawney went still further. He could not accept that even equality of income was true equality. He could accept it only as a means to an end. For the saintly Tawney the only equality which was worth fight-

ing for was equality of regard. Equality of income was only worth
having if it led to equality of regard. He saw this as the central purpose
of the Labour Party.

> Its fundamental dogma is the dignity of man; its fundamental
> criticism of capitalism is, not merely that it impoverishes the mass
> of mankind – poverty is an ancient evil – but that it makes riches
> a God, and treats common men as less than men. Socialism accepts
> therefore, the principles, which are the corner-stones of democracy,
> that authority to justify its title, must rest on consent; that power is
> tolerable only so far as it is accountable to the public; and that
> differences of character and capacity between human beings, how-
> ever important on their own plane, are of minor significance com-
> pared with the capital fact of their common humanity. Its object
> is to extend the application of these principles from the sphere of
> civil and political rights, where, at present, they are nominally
> recognized, to that of economic and social organization, where they
> are systematically and insolently defied. The socialist movement and
> the Labour Party exists for that purpose.[19]

An interesting feature of this equality of regard separates it from the
other kinds of equality. In the other cases we have more or less clear
and readily comprehensible abstract descriptions; but equality of
regard is less easy to grasp. But – and this surely is the fascinating
thing about it – equality of regard is easier to describe. Steven Lukes
has recently collected some such descriptions from within the British
Labour movement. His list is evocative:

> This denial of autonomy was what William Godwin had in mind
> when he urged universal and equal political participation on the
> grounds that 'Each man will thus be inspired with a consciousness
> of his own importance, and the slavish feelings that shrink up the
> soul in the presence of an imagined superior, will be unknown'. It is
> what William Morris meant when he wrote of socialism as a
> 'condition of equality' in which a man 'would no longer take his
> position as the dweller in such an office, or (as now) the owner of
> such and such property, but as being such and such a man'. It is
> what Tawney intended when he wrote of an egalitarian society as
> one in which 'money and position count for less, and the quality of
> human personalities for more', and what George Orwell was think-
> ing of when he wrote of 'breathing the air of equality' in revolu-
> tionary Spain, with 'no boss-class, no menial-class, no beggars, no
> prostitutes, no lawyers, no priests, no boot-licking, no cap-
> touching'.[20]

The revisionist position recognised the importance of the equality of regard. Indeed, Crosland has an entire chapter in *The Future of Socialism* which points to the insufficiency of the notion of 'equality of opportunity'. None the less the equalities which Crosland's reforms were aimed at establishing were equality of opportunity and equality of income. But equality of income cannot plausibly be made an end in itself without becoming entirely negative – 'take it away from the rich'; and, if that is all it is, it is hard to see the difference between it and jealousy. The virtue of equality of income can be seen only when the notion is tied to a further notion of the equal dignity of all men – and this the revisionists did not think out.

Two observations need to be added to these remarks. The first is an expansion of Professor Hobsbawm's criticism of the revisionist position. Hobsbawm has noted that the concept Crosland was using was entirely different from the equality of regard characteristic of some groups of workers – miners most prominently. Hobsbawm asserted that the revisionists' equality was entirely illegitimate : 'When Gaitskell and the Gaitskellites said socialism was about equality, what they meant was that it wasn't about socialism.'[21] The miners' equality is a respect each for every other, based on their common labour and exposure to danger. Their intense comradeliness is characteristic of the ethos of a number of working-class crafts. They salute the dignity of labour, especially the labourer who works at the same thing they work at.* This dignity is characteristic of crafts whose members by virtue of their work are isolated from the rest of the world, hence it is prevalent amongst miners, some groups of farm labourers, and ship-builders. The prevalence of this feeling gives some scope for the claim that 'equality' is a legitimate abbreviation of working-class practice, save that the feeling of comradeliness rarely extends beyond a specific craft. In a way which recalls the 'heroic' depictions of workers so characteristic of Soviet painting and Western revolutionary sects' banners, Hobsbawm and Tawney are legitimately abstracting from the experience of working people.

Secondly, I suspect that the revisionists' relative silence about equality of regard is no accident. Equality of regard presumes a large degree of freedom for individual men. There is thus something radically inappropriate about evolving policies to administer it. The Labour Party's role is entirely negative and preparatory; it clears the ground. It can merely remove obstacles to human freedom. In this respect, then, I think, Crosland's silence actually makes more sense

---

*A colleague tells me that he recently gave a talk on 'democracy' to a group of dockers at a conference sponsored by the National Dock Labour Board.   After his paper one docker told him, with support from his friends, that dockers were 'God's chosen people' (his phrase) and that that was what 'democracy' was all about.

than Tawney's hopes. Tawney's Labour Party is to be in the impossible position of imposing equality of regard. Tawney, truth be known, was a natural teacher. Some of the central images about the realisation of equality in *Equality* are, in a Platonic way, tutorial images. The party and the state are cast in the role of teacher or doctor. To my eye the central passage of the book is:

It [equality of provision] is to be achieved, not by treating different needs in the same way, but by devoting equal care to ensuring that they are met in the different ways appropriate to them as is done by a doctor who prescribes different regimes for different constitutions, or a teacher who developes different types of intelligence by different curricula.[22]

Elsewhere he observes: 'Progress depends, indeed, on a willingness on the part of the mass of mankind – and we all, in nine-tenths of our nature, belong to the mass – to recognise genuine superiority, and to submit themselves to its influence.'[23] And again: 'It is not a question, of course, or any mystical theory of industrial self-government, but of conferring on common men as much power as is needed to protect them against economic oppression.'[24] In this view the Labour Party is to impose equality of regard; it is the doctor, the teacher, the conferrer of power. Such conferring is incoherent. The Labour Party can, at best, be an ally of the working class in its attempt to establish equality of regard, and a minor ally at that.

For the attainment of equality – especially equality of regard – by unequal means is an illusion. No one can be given equality; equality of respect least of all. Equality, between individuals or classes, cannot be a gift – or an imposition – for the act of giving imposes obligations on the recipient; repeated one-sided giving serves nicely to remind both giver and receiver who is boss. Hence the futility of the notion that the Labour Party can use Parliament to *give* equality to the working class. Equality – between classes certainly, and also between people – can only be established from an earlier inequality if it is first *taken* and subsequently re-established whenever threatened. The price of quality, it might be said, is eternal class-struggle. Emphatically, that struggle must be between the principals on the ground crucial to both; not between the bourgeoisie on the one hand and the parliamentary-bourgeois friends of the working class on the other. Thus equality is not about the ending of conflict, or about generous, gentle, Christian gift-giving, it is about struggle. In this struggle each side must look to its own strength – to the sources of its real power.

III

If we restrict the contention that socialism is about equality to the two senses of equality – equality of opportunity and equality of income – which parliamentary action might bring about, can we reasonably say that Labour governments have succeeded in producing a more egalitarian Britain? It was all but universally believed in the early fifties that Labour in 1945–51 had succeeded.

The belief that the provisions of the welfare state combined with steeply progressive direct (income) taxation had 'levelled out' society was accepted on the basis of rather slim evidence because it was useful for the leaders of both major parties to believe it. The evidence was found in two sources: a study of poverty amongst working-class families in York conducted by B. Seebohm Rowntree and G. R. Lavers and published by them in a diminutive volume, *Poverty and the Welfare State: A Third Social Survey of York Dealing Only with Economic Questions* (1951), and the *92nd Annual Report of the Board of Inland Revenue* published in October 1950. The findings of these studies pointed in a similar direction.

Rowntree and Lavers chose York because York was widely accepted as a microcosm of British society; because it was small enough to survey with limited resources; and, most importantly, because similar surveys had been conducted there at the turn of the century and in 1939. The earlier surveys would provide some interesting comparative data. Rowntree and Lavers took the measures of poverty used by their predecessors and adjusted them to take account of inflation and other external changes which had occurred since 1936. It is important to be clear that their notion of poverty was austere in the extreme. To be poor in their sense was not to have a dry place to live and/or enough calories and vitamins to sustain a healthy life. The severity of the standard was dictated to them by their attempt to get information comparable with their predecessors'. This point is of considerable import later on as much less severe notions of poverty are invoked today. Some idea of just how severe their standards were can be gleaned from the fact that they did not seek to interview working-class people ('working-class' was defined by income) who were institutionalised (i.e. in hospitals, old people's homes, etc.) on the ground that by definition such people could not have been poor – they had a dry bed, some clothes and regular meals; or, again, that they made no attempt to adjust their income figures upwards to take account of the economic benefit of the free medical service available to all in 1950 because prior to the introduction of the national health service these families would have made no use of medical facilities at all.[25]

Invoking these severe standards, they discovered a 'remarkable decrease in poverty between 1936 and 1950'.[26] Moreover, the poverty that remained was highly concentrated amongst specific categories of the population: 'poverty is due to one or other of five causes . . . sickness 21·3%; old age 67·1%; death of chief wage-earner 6·3%; large number of children 3·2%; low wages 1·1%'.[27] Rowntree and Lavers attributed this improvement to a number of factors, the most important of them being the various provisions of the welfare state: 'whereas the proportion of the working class population living in poverty had been reduced since 1936 from 31·1% to 2·77% it would have been reduced to 22·18% if welfare legislation had remained unaltered'.[28] These figures were generally taken, by Tawney amongst others, to justify the welfare state and more particularly socialism's role in bringing it about.[29] This general acceptance ignored a few significant caveats which Rowntree and Lavers punctiliously entered: that the ending of widespread unemployment played an important role in keeping families out of poverty;[30] that, even so, in 10 per cent of households where the husband was in full employment the wife worked, too, and her earnings were often essential in keeping the family above the poverty line;[31] and, most important, that although very few were actually poor at any one moment a significantly higher proportion were very little above the poverty line and an even greater proportion could reasonably expect to be near this subsistence condition at some time in their lives.[32]

The general impression of an improvement at the bottom of the income scale was complemented by the comments of the Inland Revenue, who had detected, in the words of the 1950 report, 'a very considerable redistribution of incomes since pre-war'.[33] This redistribution was particularly marked when 'net incomes after tax' were considered. Table 1, taken from the BIR report, speaks for itself.

Table 1   *Classification of Income, by Ranges of Net Income after tax*

Range of Net Income	1938–9 Number of Incomes	1948–9 Number of Incomes
£ 135 – 150	2,508,000	1,113,000
150 – 250	4,630,000	8,500,000
250 – 500	1,940,000	9,152,000
500 – 1,000	507,000	1,551,000
1,000 – 2,000	142,200	349,000
2,000 – 4,000	54,640	79,650
4,000 – 6,000	11,600	5,264
over 6,000	6,560	86

Once this evidence was publicly available its political import was exploited – for more than it was worth. In retrospect the exploiters sound decidedly shrill.[35] *The Economist*, chief proponent of the view that the middle class was being squeezed out of existence, was shrillest of all. Indeed, *The Economist* didn't wait for the publication of the evidence. It began bemoaning the fate of the middle class as far back as 1947. The agony was awful:

> There has been no attempt to analyse the consequences of such a sudden wrenching of the social mechanism, with all that it implies in the removal of incentives. . . . There has been no attempt to base the changes on the merits of those who have gained or on the demerits of those who have lost; the sentimental assumption has simply been made that anyone who is paid by the week is always noble and right, while anyone who is paid by the month is inevitably an exploiter.[36]

Little enough has changed since.

R. M. Titmuss, writing in 1962, showed panistakingly that the BIR evidence was mathematically unsound. There were any number of collectively important ways in which increased benefits to the middle class did not show up in the income statistics; trusts and various other legal devices permitted people to pass on large sums of capital from generation to generation untouched, and largely unnoticed, by the dreaded Inland Revenue; certainly there was no case for the popular notion that a natural law was at work levelling incomes in the welfare state.[37] The York study was more easily dismissed as its standards of poverty were manifestly too low.

But, if the evidence of Rowntree and Lavers and the Inland Revenue cannot now be used to demonstrate the contention that the Labour government of 1945–51 had reduced inequality, the politically important fact was that it was so used during the 1950s and early 1960s, and was accepted and used to divide parties. The Conservatives and the Liberals began, hesitatingly at first, to follow the lines laid down by *The Economist* and attacked the position built up by Labour to 1951. The attack was heard from a member of the Bow Group – 'Conservatives must strive for a large reduction, in the long run, of the public services' – and from a leading Liberal economist – 'The true object of the welfare state, for the Liberal, is to teach people how to do without it'.[38] The Labour Party defended the new position. Those new provisions which were not attacked, such as the Education Act (1944), were not defended and remained uncontroversial for some time. In defending those parts of the welfare state which were attacked, the Labour Party discovered a new role for itself: in addition to being the defender of the trade unions it was now also the defender of the welfare state and, through it, of the poor.

This new role was discovered remarkably quickly and, such are the dialectical pulls of politics, accepted increasingly by both sides. The Conservative and Liberal parties could have argued that the main provisions of the welfare state – universal secondary education, the free health service and comprehensive welfare insurance – were the product of wartime unity and not just of socialism. Some, indeed, in both these parties took that, historically accurate, line. But the opponents of these provisions in both parties had the upper hand, so that the political credit (and blame) for the new provisions now attaches to the party who in government enacted them.

Did the standard of living of the poorest sections of society rise in the period between 1939 and 1949? Undoubtedly it did – and continues to do so – but the standard of living improved for all. Evidence of the improvement in living standards for all sections of society is easily come by. The height and weight of children has risen;[39] infant-mortality rates are down; the age of school leaving has risen;[40] the share of the national wage-bill going to the lowest decile has remained constant (since 1886) while the level of earnings has risen considerably;[41] and the absolute level of use of hospitals made by all classes has increased since 1948.[42] Such evidence about the rise in the absolute level of income for the poorest sections tells us, of course, nothing at all about their relative position; but it does serve, at very least, to suggest that there is no effective law of capitalism tending to the increasing impoverishment of the poorest. I hope there is nobody who wishes there were.

Since the early 1960s several lines of attack against the apparent advantages of the welfare state have developed. It is said that much more needs to be done. Abel-Smith and Titmuss have argued that middle-class people have made disproportionate use of the services of the welfare state, of the free health service and the more expensive kinds of schooling (especially university education).[43] The Child Poverty Action Group, most prominently, has shown that the number of people in poverty has risen dramatically since the mid-1960s. Various authors have argued that our notion of poverty has to be raised as expectations and the cost of living rise.[44] It can no longer be seriously claimed (though I know of no social democrat who ever did claim it) that there is a natural economic law in operation equalising incomes;[45] and, it is evident that the 1964–70 Labour government was retrogressive in this area.[46]

It is noticeable, especially in the criticism levelled at the 1964–70 Labour government, that the proponents of greater equality of income – the CPAG and other similar pressure-groups – have, in effect, accepted the social democrats' claim. Townsend and Bosanquet remark in the introduction to their well-known collection of essays, *Labour and Inequality*: 'The book does not pretend to deal with Tory policies.' Of course not: these pressure-groups expect more of a Labour government. Thus, we see that both those who are in favour of more equality and those who are opposed to it expect Labour to defend and extend the laws and practices which are aimed at inducing it. At this level we encounter a dimension of practice in which the social democrats are right: Labour is about equality in that it lives in a national political environment in which others expect it to be about equality. This expectation seems to transcend the lack of evidence that Labour has created a more equal Britain.

Indeed, one of the most revealing things about inequality of wealth and income is how little we know about it. We have facts and figures about the things we care about measuring. Our considerable ignorance about the distribution of wealth and income is, therefore, a sign that as a society we do not take financial inequality terribly seriously. In 1970, one authority on the subject, A. B. Atkinson, concluded:

> In the introduction to *Income Distribution and Social Change*, Titmuss draws attention to the reliance that has been placed on the trends in the degree of inequality shown by the Inland Revenue statistics. It was on the basis of these, for example, that Sir Edward Boyle stated in the House of Commons, in 1961, that 'we have a better and fairer distribution of incomes today than we had 10 or 11 years ago'. This view is shared by many others, although Professor Titmuss' study has undoubtedly given pause to its advocates. From the present discussion, it will, I hope, be clear that in our existing state of knowledge it is impossible to draw any such firm conclusions.[47]

It was partly to remedy this ignorance that the government established a Royal Commission on the Distribution of Income and Wealth, under the chairmanship of Lord Diamond, in August 1974. In recognition of the paucity of reliable and comprehensive information, the Royal Commission was asked, most exceptionally, to accept a standing reference on its subject, i.e. it was to prepare and publish analyses from time to time.

Thanks to the Royal Commission's first Report (in July 1975) we are in a somewhat better position than we were with comprehensive schools to measure changes over time. In the case of the schools, we do not know if there has been any change in the performance of various categories of students. The first Report of the Diamond Commission tentatively suggests that the distribution of income changed sharply in the direction of greater equality between 1938 and 1949. It continued to change after 1949, but at a slower pace. Between 1938 and 1949 the share of income held by the top 1 per cent fell by over a third (from 17·1 to 10·6 per cent) and that of the top 10 per cent by a fifth (from 40·5 to 32·1 per cent). The overall picture is conveyed in Table 2.

Diamond's first Report also showed that personal wealth (which is even more difficult to measure than income) is very much less evenly distributed than income. In 1973, half the personal wealth was owned by the richest 5 per cent of the adult population. Here, too, however, the extremes have been reduced over time. But here, as with educational policy, it is not possible yet to apportion praise and blame. The distribution of wealth (problems of interpretation aside) is affected by many factors. We are far from being able to say whether or not successive Labour governments have made much difference.

IV

It should now be obvious that the revisionists' argument that 'socialism is about equality' is not sufficiently well worked out for us to say whether or not it is reasonable. For one thing, even the fullest version of their position, Anthony Crosland's *The Future of Socialism*, is indefinite about what it means by 'equality'. The kind of equality which it takes most seriously is equality of income, yet it produces no defensible argument for the belief that this kind of equality is desirable in itself. Crosland also overestimates the extent to which the socialist tradition is about this – or any – kind of equality, and he is, to put it at its best, generous in crediting the Labour Party with having done much about this kind of equality.

The weakness of Crosland's position is also evident from the fact that some of the things Labour has done to end inequality – the creation of a comprehensive system of state education, for example – cannot be explained as a result of a determination to end inequalities of income. This is so despite the fact that Crosland raised the problem of schooling anew after the 1944 Act. The greatest sentiments for that policy are, in so far as they are understandable as principles at all, the determination to do away with the inequalities of regard which attach to the former students of the various more or less prestigious schools, and the desire to increase the opportunities for working-class boys to get middle-class jobs.

Part of Crosland's problem, it is clear, is that his statement about Labour's aims tries to cover too much ground. The party and the movement are not a coherent whole, and in many ways are becoming less so. For their part, the various trade unions have shown little enough sign of even agreeing amongst themselves as to what kind of policies – let alone what kind of society – they want. Partly, of course, what they want changes with changing external circumstances. But, while there can be no denying that some unions are supported by groups of workers for whom equality of regard is a real part of their lives, they manifestly do not (yet?) extend that comradeship to others.

Table 2 Distribution of Personal Income – Survey of Personal Incomes

Percentage shares of income, before and after income tax, received by given quantile groups; 1938/39 to 1972/73

United Kingdom

Income unit: tax unit

Quantile group	Before income tax					Income range 1972/73 (lower limit)	After income tax					Income range 1972/73 (lower limit)
	1938/39	1949/50	1959/60	1964/65	1972/73		1938/39	1949/50	1959/60	1964/65	1972/73	
	%	%	%	%	%	£ p.a.	%	%	%	%	%	£ p.a.
Top 1 per cent	17·1	10·6	7·9	7·7	6·0	7,233	11·7	5·8	4·8	5·0	4·0	5,003
2-5 ,, ,,	14·4	12·5	10·8	10·6	9·9	3,855	13·6	10·9	9·7	9·5	8·9	3,070
6-10 ,, ,,	9·0	9·0	8·7	8·7	8·8	3,109	9·3	9·0	8·6	8·5	8·5	2,565
Top 10 per cent	40·5	32·1	27·4	27·0	24·7	3,109	34·6	25·7	23·1	23·0	21·4	2,565
11-20 ,,	11·9	13·2	13·8	13·9	14·2	2,533	12·7	13·7	14·2	14·2	14·3	2,131
21-30 ,,	8·8	10·6	11·6	11·7	12·0	2,172	9·6	11·1	12·2	12·3	12·3	1,873
31-40 ,,	7·3	9·0	10·2	10·1	10·5	1,922	{27·7	{33·5	10·7	10·8	10·8	1,654
41-50 ,,	6·5	8·0	9·0	9·1	9·3	1,696			9·6	9·5	9·6	1,470
51-60 ,,	5·8	7·0	7·9	7·9	8·2	1,481			8·4	8·2	8·4	1,284
61-70 ,,	5·3	6·3	6·9	6·8	7·0	1,256			7·2	7·2	7·3	1,099
71-80 ,,	{13·8	{13·8	{13·4	5·6	5·8	1,033	{15·4	{15·9	{14·5	6·1	6·3	927
81-90 ,,				4·5	4·7	809				4·9	5·3	765
91-100 ,,				3·4	3·7	595				3·8	4·3	—

Difference as a percentage of the median between:										
highest and lowest deciles	—	—	—	139	136	—	—	—	128	122
upper and lower quartiles	62	69	71	72	71	—	—	68	69	67
Median £ p.a.	£184	£308	£621	£849	£1,696	—	—	£585	£780	£1,470
Number of tax units covered (millions)	9·8	20·1	20·7	21·1	20·3	9·8	20·1	20·7	21·1	20·3

Source: Derived from SP1.
Note. In some years the income share of some quantile groups cannot be estimated with any degree of confidence as the published range-tables have too few income ranges to permit successful interpolation.[48]

Furthermore, much of their practice is better understood as a desire
to dominate their own industries – for power, that is, not for equality
with anyone in anything.
There is an important ambiguity here. Most of the time unions
work to improve, or at least to prevent the depression of, their members' incomes. In the straightforward language of the American trade
union leader George Meany, what they want is 'More'. To act on
behalf of their members is their job. But there is more to their
economic outlook than simply preserving their differentials over those
groups immediately beneath them, or trying to prevent any widening
of the differential between their own group and that next above;
there is also a general antipathy to wealth (as opposed to income).
There is a general feeling that the comfortable standard of living of
those who have inherited (as opposed to earned for themselves) their
money is unjustifiable. It is when this aspect of their attitude to income
and wealth inequality is to the fore that the trade unions and the
Labour Party can be strongly egalitarian about wealth. Labour Party
annual conferences have passed numerous resolutions calling for a
wealth tax, or increased taxes on inheritances, or increased income
taxes on the higher incomes. But there is something abstract and
vague about this kind of egalitarianism; it lacks the punch of the day-
to-day fight to maintain one's own position.
To the extent that trade unions succeed in defending their own
members, those groups in society who cannot be, or are not, organised
lose out. This is an increasingly serious problem for the egalitarian
position because there is now much evidence to show that the poorest
people in Britain are to be found in these groups: the handicapped,
the elderly and the unemployed. It is easy to be unfair to the trade
unions here. In acting on their members' behalf, in doing their job,
they do nothing dishonourable. Moreover, there are some impressive
examples of the TUC exceeding its brief on behalf of the poor
outside its ranks. In 1976, for example, the TUC – through the TUC–
government liaison committee – pressed for the introduction of the
Child Benefit Scheme after the Cabinet had decided to postpone it.
The government had feared that the scheme, which would in effect
transfer children's allowances from husbands to wives, would be highly
unpopular with working men and would lead to inflationary wage-
demands.[49] The TUC, through the liaison committee, persuaded the
government otherwise, and a modified version of the Child Benefit
Scheme was introduced. But such examples are too few; and there are
too many examples on the other side. One practice which has recurred
recently concerns the Job Creation Scheme. No proposal to create jobs
under this scheme can be sanctioned without the approval of the
relevant trade union; all too often, unions have vetoed proposals for
work which patently will not be done by anyone if it is not done

under this scheme because some of their members might, hypothetically, do it.

The willingness of individual trade unions to act as pressure-groups raises important political problems for the revisionists. With the trade unions ranged against them it is hard to see who is going to provide the political support for egalitarianism. Without political support the egalitarian doctrine is as much an albatross around the Labour Party's neck as ever the Bevanites' socialism was. Egalitarianism can be turned to the Labour Party's electoral disadvantage. The party of equality can be attacked on grounds of high principle by the party of freedom. Some may doubt the right of the Conservative Party to pose as the party of freedom and argue that the freedom that it seeks is all too patently the freedom of the rich to exploit the rest. But no one can deny the positive value which attaches to freedom in our culture and the consequent temptation of Labour's opponents to pose as the parties of freedom when Labour's egalitarianism looks as if it can be bought only at the price of an important decrease in the freedom of all. This is not to argue for the abandonment of Labour's commitment to equality. It is simply to point out that the commitment – whether it is to the form given to it by Crosland, or to some other form – has a political price.

In many respects, the political difficulties which the revisionists have had to face have been increasing in recent years. The attitudes of Labour governments to unemployment show this dramatically. Full employment or, rather, postwar governments' commitment to full employment, was the bedrock of Labour's economic policy. This commitment was, in turn, important to the Labour Party's record on equality because a full-employment policy does much for 'equality of regard'. It may make little difference to equality of income, because the difference between the incomes of badly paid employed men and unemployed men receiving various welfare benefits – particularly if they have families – can be small. But a man who is unemployed is not a worker; he is unlikely to be self-confident or to be respected by others. Between the end of the Second World War and the inauguration of the Labour government of 1974, Britain had maintained a full-employment policy. It had been committed to this policy even at the cost of a rather higher rate of inflation than it might have without full employment. This commitment did not arise out of a new-found beneficence of capital; and it made quite a change from the prewar position. The number of unemployed people in Britain between the wars was never less than 1,000,000 in any month; it did not fall as low as a million until December 1940. For several years during the 1930s it was up to 3 million. After the war (with the sole exception of February 1947) the annual average monthly figure was never above a million (the peak was 885,500 in 1972) before the depression of 1976.

The position has been degenerating dramatically since then. The number of registered unemployed in Britain rose above the million mark in February 1976 and has never come down below it since. In December 1977, it was 1,419,700. But the absolute figure is misleading because there are now so many more people in the labour market. Figures which show the proportion of the work-force out of work since 1948 give a fairer, though thoroughly depressing, picture (see Table 3).

Table 3   *Proportion of the work-force out of work 1948–77*[50]

	%		%		%
1948	— 1·6	1958	— 2·1	1968	— 2·4
1949	— 1·5	1959	— 2·2	1969	— 2·4
1950	— 1·5	1960	— 1·6	1970	— 2·5
1951	— 1·2	1961	— 1·5	1971	— 3·4
1952	— 2·0	1962	— 2·0	1972	— 3·8
1953	— 1·6	1963	— 2·5	1973	— 2·6
1954	— 1·3	1964	— 1·6	1974	— 2·6
1955	— 1·1	1965	— 1·4	1975	— 4·3
1956	— 1·2	1966	— 1·5	1976	— 5·6
1957	— 1·4	1967	— 2·4	1977	— 6·1

The change to a policy of full employment was made possible, in the first instance, by the war. It was maintained by Conservative administrations from 1951 only after it had been made respectable by Keynes, and laid as a foundation-stone of the welfare state by Beveridge. But there can be no doubt that full employment was maintained by successive governments, particularly Conservative governments, because of the heavy political price which the Labour movement in general, and the trade unions in particular, attached to it. While it lasted this policy was a real gain for the 'equality of regard' – irrespective of the reasons for which it was actually maintained.

For many years the position in Britain has contrasted interestingly to that in the United States. There governments are not pressed, to anything like the same extent, by a united labour movement for a full-employment policy. American trade unionists, bereft of an alternative economic or political principle to that of American capital, and lacking the solidarity of the British trade union movement, acquiesce in much higher rates of unemployment than would be tolerated here. The figures for comparison are, of course, misleading. The American figures are more accurate: they show a rate that since 1965 has never been less than 3·5 per cent (in 1969) and is often nearer 5·5 per cent. The American figures can be more accurate because of the lower political sensitivity to unemployment in that country. If the British government used the American system of calculating, the British figures would be higher – though still lower than the American figures. Which government is going to be that honest? However one calculates, the British figures are lower than the American for comparable years and much lower than before the Labour Party had ever formed a majority administration.

As can be seen from the table above, the British rate of unemployment has worsened rapidly in the years since 1965. In that year it was 1·6 per cent; in 1977 it was 6·1 per cent. Labour was in office for the greater part of this time. No one, I think, would attribute rising unemployment entirely to the Labour governments of those years. The causes are deep-seated. Perhaps they are intractable. What is noticeable, however, for this discussion about the Labour Party's attitude to equality is that the party has reduced its commitment to full employment. It has been allowed by its allies in the trade union movement to place a higher price on protecting the security of those who still have jobs, and on keeping down the rate of inflation, than on trying to get the rate of unemployment down. This change of priority has been evident in a number of the actions of the 1974 government. It chose to protect jobs (and give employers a small additional disincentive to taking on additional labour) through its Employment Protection Act. It imposed cuts in the rate of public expenditure and thereby reduced the number of jobs in local authorities and in the building industry in 1975 and 1976.

The change of heart which these policies mark has many causes. One of them is an abandonment of the Keynesian belief in growth and in the beneficence of growing rates of public expenditure. These beliefs, hardly the stuff of revolutionary socialism, underwrote the optimism of C. A. R. Crosland's egalitarianism. I have pointed in this chapter to some of the intellectual weaknesses and political difficulties which that doctrine faced. I have not done this in any spirit of disrespect. On the contrary, I believe that the egalitarian doctrine possessed a nobility and humanity which will not be easy to replace now that it is so discredited.

NOTES

1 See Drucker, H. M., *The Political Uses of Ideology* (London, 1974), pt. 3.
2 Crosland, C. A. R., *Socialism and Other Essays* (London, 1974), p. 15, also p. 124. Some commentators have taken him literally. See Parkin, F., *Class Inequality and Political Order: Social Stratification in Capitalist and Communist Societies* (London, 1972), p. 114.
3 See, for example, Jay, D., *The Socialist Case* (London, 1937). Gaitskell, H., 'Public ownership and equality', *Socialist Commentary*, vol. 19, June 1955, pp. 165–7, and *Socialism and Nationalisation*, Fabian Tract no. 300, July 1956. Jenkins, R., 'Equality', in Crossman, R. H. S. (ed.), *New*

Fabian Essays (London, 1962), pp. 69–90. Mackintosh, J. P., 'Socialism or social democracy? The choice for the Labour Party', *Political Quarterly*, vol. 43, no. 4, 1972, pp. 470–84.

4   Gaitskell, 'Public ownership and equality', p. 166.
5   Crosland, *Socialism*, p. 17.
6   Abrams, M., Rose, R., and Hinden, R., *Must Labour Lose?* (Harmondsworth, 1960).
7   ibid., p. 36. The whole survey was based on a sample of 724; pp. 9–10. If nationalisation was ever popular, it had lost its edge as early as July 1949; see Addison, P., *The Road to 1945* (London, 1975).
8   Abrams, Rose, Hinden, *Must Labour Lose?* p. 48.
9   ibid., p. 53.
10   ibid., p. 58.
11   ibid., p. 97. The authors, however, did not accept the 'affluent workers' thesis fully.
12   ibid., p. 100.
13   ibid., p. 100.
14   ibid., p. 58.
15   Crossman, R. H. S., *New Fabian Essays* (London, 1962).
16   Jenkins, R., 'Hugh Gaitskell: a political memoir', *Encounter*, No. 125, February 1964, p. 8.
17   Haseler, S., *The Gaitskellites: Revisionism in the British Labour Party 1951–64* (London, 1969), p. 172.
18   The most up-to-date survey of the arguments and the evidence is to be found in Wright, N., *Progress in Education* (London, 1977), ch. 4.
19   Tawney, R. H., *Equality* (London, 1964 edn), p. 197.
20   Lukes, S., 'Socialism and equality', in Kolakowski, L., and Hampshire, S., *The Socialist Idea: A Reappraisal* (London, 1974), p. 79. Lukes is somewhat unfair to the revisionists. He accuses Crosland of being interested in the 'equality of opportunity' to the exclusion of 'equality of respect'. Crosland has an entire chapter which points to the insufficiency of the notion of 'equality of opportunity'. Parkin, *Class Inequality*, makes a similar mistake, p. 122. See Crosland, *The Future of Socialism*, pp. 150–69.
21   Hobsbawm, E. J., in 'Whatever happened to equality? Equality in the party', in conversation with John Vaizey, *The Listener* 9 May 1974, p. 597. It is characteristic of this debate that Vaizey simply ignored the import of Hobsbawm's remarks. From the *Listener* script it seems that Vaizey did not take in what Hobsbawm had said. It must be remembered, however, that the *Listener* article was an edited version of a broadcast tape.
22   Tawney, *Equality*, pp. 49–50.
23   ibid., p. 87. Crosland agrees: see *Future of Socialism*, pp. 118*ff*.
24   Towney, *Equality*, p. 180.
25   Rowntree, B. Seebohm, and Lavers, G. R., *Poverty and the Welfare State: A Third Social Survey of York Dealing only with Economic Questions* (London, 1951), p. 44.
26   ibid., p. 32.
27   ibid., p. 34.
28   ibid., p. 40.
29   Towney, R. H., *The Radical Tradition* (twelve essays on politics, education and literature by Tawney edited by Rita Hinden) (Harmondsworth, 1966), p. 179.
30   Rowntree, and Lavers, *Poverty*, p. 45.
31   ibid., pp. 55, 57.

32 ibid., p. 80.
33 Quoted in Titmuss, R. M., *Income Distribution and Social Change: A Study in Criticism* (London, 1962), pp. 16, 25.
34 *Ninety-Second Annual Report of the Board of Inland Revenue* (for the year ended 31 March 1949), Cmd 8052, p. 83.
35 See John Saville's account. Saville, J., 'Labour and income distribution', in Miliband, R., and Saville, J. (eds), *The Socialist Register 1965*, pp. 147–62.
36 Quoted in ibid., p. 151.
37 Titmuss, *Income Distribution*, p. 197.
38 Quoted in Marshall, T. H., *Social Policy in the Twentieth Century* (London, 1975), pp. 102–3.
39 See Rowntree and Lavers, *Poverty*, p. 95.
40 This evidence is summarised in Field, F., *Unequal Britain: A Report on the Cycle of Inequality* (London, 1974), pp. 19–20.
41 ibid., p. 26.
42 ibid., pp. 43–8.
43 Abel-Smith, B., and Titmuss, R. M., *The Cost of the National Health Service* (Cambridge, 1956), pp. 149ff. See also Titmuss, R. M., *Essays on 'The Welfare State'* (London, 1974), ch. 2.
44 See, for example, Runcimann, W. G., 'Occupational class and the assessment of economic inequality in Britain', in Wedderburn, D., *Poverty, Inequality and Class Structure* (Cambridge, 1974), pp. 93–108.
45 Frank Parkin, for one, has refuted the claim which has not been made. His account also suffers from assuming the existence in some mythical past of an extremist Labour Party. Parkin, *Class Inequality and Political Order*, ch. 4.
46 Townsend, P., and Bosanquet, N., *Labour and Inequality* (London, 1972), p. 6.
47 Atkinson, A. B., 'Poverty and income equality in Britain', in Wedderburn, *Poverty*, pp. 67–8.
48 *First Report of the Royal Commission on the Distribution of Income and Wealth* (July 1975), p. 36.
49 See, Field, F., 'Killing a commitment: Cabinet v. the children', *New Society*, 24 June 1976.
50 Department of Employment and Productivity, *British Labour Statistics: Historical Abstract* (London, 1971), table 165, p. 316; and *British Labour Statistics Yearbook 1975* (London, 1977), table 89, p. 220.

4
Labour's Doctrines: Socialism without Planning?

I

Socialism has many doctrines. It has gained breadth by picking up interesting and important parts of various of the nineteenth- and twentieth-century schools of thought. In picking up strands as diverse as egalitarianism, rationalism, anarchism, romanticism and Marxism it has become an unwieldy ideology – an easy target for criticism.[1] Its catholicity is actually a sign of strength, not a source of weakness. No ideology is a coherent, philosophically respectable whole. It cannot be; the uneasy practical business of propagation, testing in practice, learning from experience and consequent change see to that. The important difference between ideologies is not between coherent and incoherent ideologies but between those which have the basic force and weight to attract new and diverse adherents and those which are forever purifying themselves by separating off 'tendencies'; the former go from strength to strength, while the latter are a nuisance. Ideologies are, this is to say, more akin to political parties than to philosophies, and the ideology of the British Labour Party is, like the party itself, a tumultuous alliance of diverse parts. To ask, as a few always will, what is the 'real socialism' in the ideology is to ask the wrong question; it is also to demonstrate an intolerant temperament, a temperament out of harmony with the ethos of the party.

That said, having examined Labour's commitment to equality in the previous chapter, I want to turn in this chapter to focus on another long-standing and important element in Labour's doctrines – its belief in the virtues of 'planning' – and suggest that many of the reasons previously advanced for accepting these virtues are now incredible, and that, consequently, an important element in the ideology has to be rethought. Labour's commitment to planning is a consequence of its commitment to parliamentary politics.

Since 1906, at least, the Labour Party has been committed to parliamentary politics; it has been committed to the long chain of reasoning which leads from working people voting Labour (and confining their political activity to voting Labour) to the establishment of socialism in Britain by a Labour government. This chain of reasoning is very important to the party, and the defence of it goes some way to explaining a number of its otherwise inexplicable beliefs. For example, the commitment to the parliamentary road goes some way to explaining the extraordinary attachment within one wing of the party to the belief in the primacy of Parliament in the government machine. Put another way: a large section of the left of the party holds firmly to nineteenth-century radical views. Aneurin Bevan, Michael Foot and Ken Coates, among others, have proudly declared their radical credentials.[2] Why should these figures on the more self-consciously socialist wing of the party proclaim their adherence to a pre-socialist view of the constitution? The answer is that they want to defend their position on two fronts – against the right of the party (who believe that the executive powers of the government have long since reduced Parliament to unimportance) and against the non-Labour left (who believe that, at the very best, Parliament is little more than a propaganda platform and that a parliamentary career is inherently a sell-out). By upholding the nineteenth-century radical view the Labour left can face both enemies in good heart. It can believe that supporting a Labour Party in the country and working for socialism in the House of Commons might succeed and are, in fact, given an intractable capitalist society, the most likely way to achieve its end.

In upholding this belief, the Labour left performs an ideological task which is useful to the entire party. For only if the party can honestly be presented to its voters as a machine which can 'turn the levers of power for working people' can it hope to keep together: keeping together is a condition of its forming even an occasional government. Without these victories the right would never get to play with its precious toys of executive power. Here is one reason for the tenacity of the commitment to nineteenth-century radical views of parliamentary control of the executive.

But belief in the control of the executive by Parliament is not enough to make socialists into good parliamentary animals. That requires a number of further and very un-nineteenth-century radical arguments. The nineteenth-century Parliament was, to our eyes, an incredibly idle place. It passed, on average, one important Bill a session. During a recent session (1974–5) Parliament passed seventy-four Bills, a number of which were of major import. Moreover, the nineteenth-century Parliament confined itself to issues to which changes in the law clearly did make a considerable difference. A Parliament can, indisputably, alter the suffrage. It can also establish or disestablish churches with certain legal privileges; it can vote money to make, or stop the making of, war; it can reform the methods of entry to the civil service. Its power in areas such as these is not in dispute. But parliamentary socialism requires a vastly more active Parliament attempting to control action over a much wider field than was attempted in the nineteenth century, and these extensions require new arguments.

It would be too much to say that socialists have tried to use Parliament to legislate for human happiness, but that has been the general aim of their specific Bills. They have tried to use Parliament to control government, society and the economy in order to raise, dramatically to raise, the sum of human happiness. It is safe to say that unless socialists thought Parliament could be put to these ends they would have no business entering it. But how to achieve it? How, given the split of society into two opposing camps, could the Labour Party, backed by the institutions and votes of the workers, use Parliament, hitherto the plaything of idle and clever members of the dominant class, to raise the sum of human happiness? By accepting Parliament for what its apologists said it was, the central power in the land, and using its power over government to control or, as it is usually somewhat less aggressively put, to *plan* society. If the Labour Party had accepted the low estimate of Parliament and government current amongst both Marxists and Liberals, it could not have proceeded on its parliamentary path. Marxists, especially the British Communist Party during the formative period of the Labour Party before its first majority government in 1945, deprecated both Parliament and government. For them Labour's path was inherently quixotic, for the overwhelming power of capital in society outside government would frustrate or crush a socialist Parliament. The Labour left – Laski, Cripps, Strachey *et al.* – spent much effort, especially in the 1930s and early 1940s, convincing themselves and others that Parliament could bring about socialism. For their part, the older parties knew well enough that Parliament had real economic power in so far as it could raise and lower tariffs, legalise trade unions, impose limitations over hours of work and such. But the notion that it might systematically set out to run the economy so as, for instance, to provide full employment was absurd and unnatural. Labour's socialism drove a new path around both these beliefs. It believed that a Labour government could control and rationally plan the economy from a power-base in Parliament.

Central to this project was a belief in planning: in the rational use of all the nation's economic resources under parliamentary scrutiny. When Labour first achieved office under its own steam the concept was fully worked out (if defensively argued). In 1947 in its Annual Economic Survey the government announced:

The object of economic planning is to use the national resources in the best interests of the nation as a whole. How this is to be done must depend upon the economic circumstances of the country, its stage of political development, its social structure and its methods of government. The proper system of economic planning for the United Kingdom must start from this fact, and cannot follow some theoretical blueprint. . . .[3]

But this belief did not spring fully formed from the government's brain. It had a history and involved a synthesis of several experiences and theories.

In the first place, Labour had not always been a *dirigiste* party. Its leaders first knew power in local government and for some time placed their hopes on 'municipal socialism'. The Webbs, for example, were impressed by the possibilities of using the London County Council (of which Sidney was a member) for advancing socialism. In 1918, when the party adopted Sidney Webb's pamphlet, *Labour and the New Social Order*, as its programme, little enough thought had been given to the means of achieving socialism. *Labour and the New Social Order* does not use the vocabulary of planning; neither does it lay down what machinery Labour would evolve in office to run the economy or such firms or industries as it might nationalise. Though the pamphlet's argument leans heavily on the contrast between the economic chaos of capitalism and a rational world under socialism, it is vague about how the change is to be effected.

By the early 1930s the situation had radically altered. Nearly every essay in Cripps' *Problems of a Socialist Government* spoke of the need for a socialist government to establish the machinery capable of planning the economy.[4] E. F. Wise, for instance, listed this task as second in importance only to nationalisation itself: 'The second objective will be the bringing into operation of a National Plan for economic development. Our great industries must be considered as services to supply the needs of the whole community and not to provide profits for private shareholders.'[5] William Mellor provided another argument for planning: 'Unemployment cannot, in fact, be cured without complete socialist planning on the basis of complete social ownership and control of wealth, production and distribution.'[6] G. D. H. Cole added that taking over the banks would be 'clearly indispensable in order to put the government in a position both to ensure an adequate supply of capital and credit, and to distribute that supply to the various industries in accordance with its general Socialist Economic Plan', and: 'Complete Socialist planning is only possible on the basis of the complete socialisation of industry. . . . We shall not be in a position to achieve that at a blow; and, therefore, we shall have to begin with an incomplete and partial economic plan. But it will be necessary to bring at once into existence the general organs of administration needed for the development of the Plan.'[7] Truly, planning had become Planning.

This change in vocabulary and emphasis, as Adrian Oldfield has shown, had become official policy in the early 1930s.[8] *For Socialism and Peace*, Labour's programme of 1934, spoke of 'the resources of the nation to be deliberately planned for attaining the maximum general well being',[9] and by 1937 Clement Atlee was proudly outlining Labour's 'Short Programme' in his *The Labour Party in Perspective*.[10] We may fairly ask what had produced the change.

The largest factor, by far, was the success and prestige which (then) attached to the first of the Soviet's Five-year Plans (1928–33). Hugh Dalton spoke for many when he asserted: 'The two outstanding examples of planning on a large scale in recent times are furnished by the World War and by the Soviet experiment.'[11] He goes on to urge: 'Clearly we must create, at an early stage, a Supreme Economic Authority.' At the same time, the Webbs wrote that they were 'induced' to travel to the Soviet Union to investigate 'the deliberate planning of all the nation's production, distribution and exchange, not for swelling the profit of the few but for increasing the consumption of the whole community'.[12] They were not disappointed by what they saw.

But there were other factors. The prolonged postwar depression was one of them. It became increasingly obvious that the ills of the economy, and the protection of the people against them, could only be solved on a national basis. It is symptomatic that the Scottish trade unions and the Scottish Labour movement as a whole forsook their previous nationalism as they realised that Scotland herself lacked the resources to cure her economic ills.[13] It was obvious, too, that George Lansbury had made his point in Poplar: local government could not be expected to pay for an adequate system of welfare when millions were unemployed for years. Salvation, if it were to be had at all, could only come from the political unit which had the resources – the central government.

To add to these factors, something had to be done about Labour's ideological weaponry after the ignominious performances of the 1924 and 1929–31 governments. If all Labour had to offer in government was the same nostrums as its opponents, it could not keep its head up. An addition to the ideology was called for. Barbara Wootton put her finger on the ideological weakness:

> It has long been a joke against socialists that they answer every question and dispose of every criticism by a reference to the 'abolition of the capitalist system', but that if pressed, they would as often as not be quite unable to explain in precise terms what

exactly was to be understood by that phrase: what were the features which made the capitalist system capitalist.

And on the stuff to fill it: 'In other words, any contrast of socialism with capitalism, of plan with no plan. . . .'[14] The ideological vacuum could be filled by the adoption of 'Planning'.[15]

To these arguments was added another, though the impact of this argument on the party (as opposed to the more vague 'progressive opinion') is in doubt – planning became a fashionable tool because it proffered an alternative method of allocating resources once capitalism and, with it, the price mechanism were destroyed. This aspect of the argument is important in the writings of G. D. H. Cole and Barbara Wootton. Lichtheim writes:

Socialists are at a minimum committed to economic planning that goes counter to the operation of an economy in which private firms predominate and profits are distributed among shareholders and managers.[16]

Lichtheim speaks, of course, not merely of British socialism in the thirties.

Before long, the commitment to a planned economy – to replacing the chaos and waste of capitalism with rational plans – came, for many, to be the very essence of socialism. It came to be the end towards which other goals, like nationalisation, were means; or, in some versions, the two goals came to be thought of as parts of the same process. Francis Williams quotes Clement Attlee saying of his 1945 policy: 'Fundamental nationalisation had got to go ahead because it fell in with the planning, the essential planning of the country.'[17] By that time the party leadership had experience of operating the wartime economy. They had, though none was to know it then, enjoyed better conditions for planning – wartime unity of purpose and the absense of any organised opposition – than they, or any subsequent socialist government, were to know (or be able to create).

As if all these reasons were not sufficient, it was also obvious that 'planning' was compatible with parliamentary politics. Establishing satisfactory planning machinery in central government was far from simple. It took far longer than the thirties' socialists seemed to expect. If we include in this machinery mechanisms to control wages and prices (as surely in logic we must), then of course we have to admit that the machinery is far from complete even today. Yet, for all the political distance which still separates us from having the complete machinery, it has always been clear that a parliamentary party in government *could* create it. Planning machinery is the casuistry of parliamentary socialism. It shows us how to move, step by step, from the present world to the ideal, and furthermore it does not threaten to destroy present gains in a revolutionary holocaust. Ramsey MacDonald's problem – how to use the existing machinery in a socialist way – was solved, or so it seemed.

II

When I first joined the Labour Party and began to meet people in it, I was struck straight away by how self-satisfied and self-confident the older members were with their party and what it had achieved. Like most young people, I put their attitude down to their age. This, I am now convinced, was only part of the truth. It is the case that Labour's older activists, to whose patient, dependable work the party owes much, *are* self-satisfied and a bit uncritical. If they were not, they could not have remained loyal. But I do not think any fair-minded person who looks back on the kind of things which Labour was working for in the decades before 1945 could deny that a good many of them have been achieved – more than might reasonably have been expected in those decades. To mention Planning: the United Kingdom now has the Public Expenditure Survey Committee – a committee of the Treasury which seeks to plan major government expenditure over the following five years; the Central Policy Review Staff – a committee within the Cabinet Office which investigates particular problems and advises government on future policy about them (Concorde, for example); Programme Analysis and Review – a method of investigating the programmes of the traditional ministries; and the National Economic Development Council – an attempt to co-ordinate the policies of government, industry and unions. Altogether a formidable array of machinery which has earned considerable praise from foreign students of public administration.[18]

But planning is only a method. Popular support attaches to things like Britain's systems of national minima for welfare benefits and to the national health service. It is also the case that Britain's economy is now dominated by the public sector – a sector which is growing relatively to the rest of the economy, so that it disposes of 54 per cent of the Gross National Product (32·4 per cent if transfer payments to individuals and other public bodies are excluded), and is growing absolutely. Because of its dominance of the economy the government is universally expected to control the rate of credit, of inflation and the rate of unemployment. So powerful is the government's position, especially in a period of rapid inflation, that it can get its way on substantial social issues simply by refusing to give inflation supplementation to its grants: in this way grant-aided schools are humbled and a more comprehensive system of schools created. All of these are changes which Labour wanted. It has got them and, on top of it all, has lived to see the nationalisation of large sections of British industry. Nationalisation, if not of whole industries, at least of important firms (Harland & Wolfe, Upper Clyde Shipbuilders, British Leyland) is now, in fact, the common practice of government; then, too, the Empire has been disbanded.

Yet the achievements have turned to ashes in the mouth, and young socialists do not care for the flavour. Why has the achievement failed? There are, it seems to me, two sorts of answer. The first is that in various ways the credit for the achievements just mentioned goes to others. The economic doctrines which taught Britain and the Labour Party the advantages of 'demand management', and with them the whole series of institutions which amount to economic planning, were learned from Liberal, not socialist, teachers.

Much is sometimes made of the fact that the 1929–31 MacDonald administration did not make use of the Keynesian ideas of the Liberal 'Yellow Book' (the programme of Lloyd George) published before the 1929 general election. Robert Skidelsky, for example, focuses on this omission in his *Politicians and the Slump*.[19] He claims that the Labour government's inaction when such valuable remedies lay close to hand was the result of the government's unwillingness to believe that anything could be done before the revolution. However, the intellectual failure of that government goes further than that. For not accepting Liberal plans, it at least had the excuse of fearing betrayal and trickery by its old enemy, Lloyd George. The real failure in that case was that very similar theories to those contained in the 'Yellow Book' were to be found within the Labour movement. The Independent Labour Party, guided by J. A. Hobson as the Lloyd-Georgeites were led by Keynes, were presenting reasonably well worked-out versions of the same ideas. The culpability of the second MacDonald government is not to be explained by an excuse of socialism but by an infirmity of will.

The truth is that Labour showed little resistance to Liberal economic doctrine. The authors of *For Socialism and Peace* learned about the operation of the multiplier from a paper by R. F. Kahn, which appeared shortly before the Labour programme.[20] Similarly, the 1945–51 government inherited a very strict system of manpower planning as well as the Keynesian system of fiscal planning from its wartime predecessor. Accordingly, as Professor Beer has observed, the *Economic Survey for 1947* set out the government's general economic objectives and then listed 'the distribution of manpower needed to achieve these objectives'.[21] The government's distinctively socialist policy required inflation to be held until manpower was built up and the production of goods which were in scarce supply increased.[22] A 'Keep Left' speaker at the 1947 conference said:

Socialist economics mean seeing and dealing with our problems as a whole in real physical terms, with all the money-juggling, all the manoeuvres for private profit, all the waste of duplicated effort, cut down to a minimum.[23]

By steps the Labour government was won away from this view. It first accepted that a budget surplus was necessary to reduce demand, then it moved away from manpower planning. The government was moving from a socialist policy to a Keynesian one; from a system which discouraged profit-making to one that depended on it. The result was not the less successful for that, but it was not socialist.

Beer quotes Herbert Morrison to the effect that one reason why Labour abandoned manpower socialist economics was 'Cabinet Government'.[24] Morrison may sometimes be accused of overstressing the importance of having the right machinery to do the job to hand, but this time he has an interesting point. In 1945, the first majority Labour government inherited machinery, part of which accorded with venerated socialist sympathies. But this machinery had not been operated in normal peacetime conditions. Not only was there no official opposition party to rally anti-government interests and encourage discontent, but there was also no need to worry about money. The value of the pound sterling had been underwritten for the duration of the war by the American government. This gave the government a blissful freedom to ignore expenditure and trade balances. The Chancellor was not even a member by right of the War Cabinet.[25] To operate a planning system of any kind, let alone the more demanding manpower planning, when this exceptional situation ended, the government would need new machinery. 'Cabinet Government' is another name for *ad hoc*, often *ad hominem*, compromise. Planning an economy, especially when one is thinking of moving large numbers of workers and their families about the country to places indicated in plans, requires long-range co-ordination of functions. With hindsight, it is clear that the brave ideas of 1945–8 required the Public Expenditure Survey Committee (PESC), Programme Analysis and Review (PAR), the National Economic Development Council (NEDC), the Central Policy Review Staff (CPRS) and much more. The Labour government ought to have seen this. Its ideologists had been saying things of this sort since 1934, but it did not heed the advice. Instead it fell back on the operation of devices of fiscal and monetary policy. Labour's shame is much the greater for the fact that when the new administrative machinery was created the impetus came from within the civil service and owed as much to Tory prime ministers as to Harold Wilson: more ashes.

Perhaps even more disillusioning to the committed Labour Party man is the recognition that other Western nations, including some which have had little or no socialist government, have a record of receptiveness to change on the kinds of thing which interested Labour before 1945 which is little different from Britain's. There is now considerable evidence to suggest, for example, that the proportion of a nation's GNP which it spends on the social services is a function of the size of the GNP, not the politics of the country. The richer spends more; the poorer less.[26] In Europe, Britain is amongst the latter.

If we had been listening, we might have heard something of the sort predicted long ago. Evan Durbin, forgotten prophet, was suggesting in 1940 that socialism was the coming vogue whatever the name of the party in power. He was particularly insistent on this in regard to the centralised control of the economy:

> Indeed [the search for security is] the most important of all the popular reactions to the insecurity of capitalism, because it is bringing slowly into existence the institutions of an economy different in kind from that now existing. It consists in a frontal attack upon the institutions of *laissez-faire* itself. The causal connection between the search for security and the disappearance of *laissez-faire* is sometimes ignored and nearly always misunderstood.
>
> The facts are familiar to, and widely lamented by the defenders of the *Ancien Régime*. The essential point is as follows: Whatever the name of the government in power and whatever its theoretical principles may be, the central control of industry, trade and finance is everywhere extending at an amazing rate.[27]

And so it was. In retrospect we must credit the early Fabians with prescience and with the basic political good sense to back a sure winner. The gradual increments in state power, and the gradual dominance in that power of a technocratic bureaucracy, were bound to break the back of *laissez-faire* sooner or later. But the price of accepting this development is a radical limitation on the amount of credit Labour can claim for its achievement.

III

There is, however, a far more serious problem about any claims Labour's foot-soldiers might want to advance on behalf of their army: the achievement of a highly centrally controlled economy with a dominant public sector has given rise to a number of difficult problems not forseen in the socialist literature. There are, of course, a number of problems associated with trying to run a mixed economy from the left. It is not at all obvious, for one thing, how a socialist government can prevent the owners of the remaining firms from running down their investments. Such firms will respond only to incentives of profitability, which a Labour government is committed to abolish. Difficulties of this kind have been lovingly embellished in communist critiques of socialism.[28] I do not wish to pass judgement on them; simply to note that the new problems I have in mind are different from those put forward by the communists. There are, of course, a good many kinds of problem which I am going to skip over lightly here. I am mainly concerned with the problems internal to socialist planning; not with merely technical problems about its implementation, nor with external problems which have bedevilled attempts to bring it to fruition in Britain. I think it is very important to see that there are problems at the very centre of the project – problems so serious than an honest parliamentary socialist must question the basis of his faith.

It might be best to list these problems:

(1) *The overloading of Parliament*

Governments of both parties, but especially Labour governments, have fallen into the habit of proposing so much legislation, and then forcing the bulk of it through Parliament, that it is difficult to believe that we any longer have parliamentary socialism. In the parliamentary session November 1974 to November 1975 the government proposed seventy-nine Bills (four were withdrawn). Most of the Bills were of little import, but a number were significant and complex: the Community Land Bill, the Employment Protection Bill, the Offshore Petroleum Development (Scotland) Bill, an Industry Bill, a Trade Union and Labour Relations Bill, to name a few.[29] A Parliament which passes so much legislation is overloaded. Of course, not all Parliaments do. The session of 1974–5 was exceptional in this regard because a newly elected government was seeking to get as much as possible of its contentious legislation enacted and operating before it had to face another election; with its tiny (later non-existent) majority this was understandable. But later sessions in the same Parliament, when the number of Bills was smaller, hardly showed Parliament in a better light. In the 1977–8 session the House of Commons allocated fourteen sittings to the committee stage of the Scotland Bill. But even this long period of consideration was inadequate; sixty-one of the Bill's eighty-three clauses were not debated at all.

In addition to its difficulties in debating legislation Parliament is now regularly approving something like 2,000 Statutory Instruments a year. In a recent report the Joint Committee on Statutory Instruments condemned the 'recurring tendency' of ministers and their departments to use this procedure to seek to bypass Parliament. According to the Joint Committee too many Statutory Instruments omit important details that the public has the right to know and too many leave wide scope for ministerial discretion. It is hard to have much respect for a Parliament which allows itself to be abused in this way. Can a parliamentary socialist long maintain that such a system is worth defending? Parliamentary control is even less satisfactory when we look at its surveillance of expenditure.[30] For a time the Expenditure Committee had fallen into the habit of demanding cuts in overall expenditure while asking for rises in specific heads of expenditure. Early in 1978 the Public Accounts Committee provoked a fight with the British Steel Corporation in order to force the Corporation to produce important information about its finances. This could have been an important victory for Parliament over the executive, but both sides backed down.

(2) *The inherent irrationality of some government expenditure*
Governments have taken over responsibility for financing some heads of expenditure about which there is no non-arbitrary way of measuring success. Some such heads are very expensive. Expenditure on the national health service is an outstanding example of this problem. In 1974–5, 4·5 per cent of the GNP was spent on the national health service. It is quite impossible to say if this is enough, or too much, because we have no criteria of success in a health service.

Dr David Owen, sometime Minister of State for Health in the 1974 government, has admitted as much. In an interview with Oliver Gillie of the *Sunday Times*, he said:

The Health Service was launched on a fallacy. First we were going to finance everything, cure the nation, and then spending would drop. That fallacy has been exposed. Then there was the period when everybody thought the public could have whatever they needed on the Health Service – it was just a question of governmental will. Now we recognise that no country, even if they where prepared to pay the taxes, can supply everything.[31]

The expenditure which could be made on the health service if all Britons used it to the full is incredible. According to one of the results of the 1973 General Household Survey, for every person who goes to the doctor many more who experience symptoms of disease do not. The survey found that only 5 per cent of the population had no symptoms. Nineteen per cent of those who had symptoms took no action, and of the 76 per cent who took some action two-thirds treated themselves.[32] It is easy to see that one reason why the health service works at all is that most people, through some combination of self-reliance, stoicism, fear or ignorance, do not enforce their right to use the service. The number of contacts between patients and general practitioners has fallen by 25 per cent since the inauguration of the national health service, according to a 1973 estimate. It is not difficult to see that a great deal more than 4·5 per cent of the GNP could be spent on this service.[33] The 4·5 per cent is spent on the 25 per cent of the population who go to their GP. More would be needed if more people went to their doctor when they felt unwell. But would that be better than 4·5 per cent? Or is 4·5 per cent enough? There are no satisfactory answers to these questions. But in what way, then, can we rationally plan health service expenditure?

The operation of the national health service provides additional examples of the problems of rationally planning government expenditure. The Halsbury Committee (1974) on nurses' pay accepted the nurses' unions' claim that the prevailing low level of salaries resulted in a 17 per cent shortfall of nurses below establishment levels.[34] The Committee recommended, and the Department of Health and Social Security accepted, a rise of 30 per cent in nurses' pay: 10 per cent to restore their previous position in the pay hierarchy and 20 per cent to attract 17 per cent more nurses. The DHSS seems not to have noticed that, if the 17 per cent did turn up for employment, the additional cost of paying them would be £170m. a year, more than the increase in the total NHS expenditure then planned for 1975–6.

The questionable part of Halsbury's logic was his acceptance of the notion that the establishment was the right number of nurses for the national health service at the time. This is an assumption shared by other bodies. The police are an example. All police constabularies are now staffed at levels lower than the establishment.[35] We are told that declining numbers of policemen are bad for the morale of those who remain: I know from personal experience in a university which is losing staff while gaining students that falling morale is a real problem in these circumstances. But that does not, surely, mean that an establishment must be maintained because it was once achieved? Since, in all these fields, we have no acceptable measure of success, we simply do not know how big the complement of staff should be.

(3) *The diversity of government responsibilities which is now so great that officials appear on both sides of specific questions*

This problem is particularly obvious in land-use planning tribunals. At the Drumbuie inquiry, the Ministry of Defence appeared against the proposal, while the Board of Trade was in favour. The decision was ultimately taken by the Secretary of State for Scotland. This example of cancelling out is not isolated. Ray Gregory has cited numerous other instances in his book, *The Price of Amenity.* Gregory cites the recurrent problem of an electricity board wanting to build a power station where a county council wants to preserve green fields.[36] Again, government is on both sides and is in the middle as well. In the last case the decision would be made by the Department of the

Environment. Examples of this kind cannot, as Professor King has recently observed, increase the authority of government.[37] On the contrary, we can begin to see the operation of a conflict between the power of government on the one hand and its authority on the other. The socialists of the thirties and forties did not see that increments in government power might be self-defeating. Consequently they could not see that increases in the powers of central government might not make planning easier at all.

Another related version of this difficulty arises in connection with government's attempts to impose controls on rises in wages and prices. Here, too, government finds itself involved on more than one side of the issue: in this case *the* politically decisive issue of the time. Government is, at once, the largest employer of labour, a dominant setter of prices (through the nationalised industries and taxation), and is yet expected as government to be above the reach of special interests. It is also expected to manage (plan) the economy to produce an ever-rising standard of goods and services. If government as employer can be forced by the industrial power of the miners to concede high wage-demands, then can it as government ask other employers and unions not to imitate it? The nationalisation of the fuel industries has not ended the struggle within those industries between unions and employer, despite some hopes to this effect amongst the socialists of the thirties and forties.

Yet another decidedly paradoxical aspect of this problem hits directly at the ability to plan rationally. In a period of accelerating inflation Treasury forecasting of the rise in its own expenditure is necessarily dishonest. A government prediction of its own future expenditure has to take into account its estimate of the likely rate of inflation in the period for which it is planning. These predictions are, of course, published. They are part of the budget and may, at least in theory, be examined in the House of Commons. Because of the scrutiny and publicity they receive, it is politically impossible for government to tell the truth about future inflation if it expects a rise. The same sort of problem applies to all politically sensitive forecasting – unemployment is another important example. Rising numbers of unemployed result in increased public expenditure for unemployment insurance and supplementary benefits as well as decreased tax revenues. The reasonable reaction to a likely rise in unemployment is to increase the revenue raised from the rest of the country. It will not happen.

(4) *The incommensurability of political and rational time*
Elections occur at least once every five years; in fact, more frequently than that. Jackson, Turner and Wilkinson have shown that British manual workers' hourly earnings (which they claim are the best simple

index of wage trends) have risen faster in the months before and immediately after general elections than otherwise. In 1970, they calculated that in the election years the average annual rate of wage-increase was 8·4 per cent, while it was only 5·9 per cent in non-election years. This is strong evidence to confirm the common suspicion that governments believe they *have to* buy off the electorate if they wish to be re-elected.[38]

The problem goes much deeper than that. The very fact of electoral politics, with its attendant change of government, is incommensurate with consistent long-term planning. New governments regularly revise the policies of their predecessors. There have been, for example, three major, different proposals for pensions since Mr Crossman produced his Pensions Bill in 1969. One of the most important points about a pension scheme is the security it gives for the long-term future to those currently in employment. For this reason a pension scheme can take a very long time to come into full effect – thirty years is sometimes necessary. How can anyone be secure when we get new schemes at the rate of one every two years?

The problems arising from changing pensions schemes, pale, however, before the problems created by rapidly changing tax schemes. Between 1964 and 1974 there were two Corporation Taxes, Capitals Grains Tax, Selective Employment Tax, Betterment Levy, Development Gains Tax, Value Added Tax, Capital Transfer Tax, Development Land Tax and Wealth Tax. The Conservative Party has already promised to repeal Wealth Tax and Capital Transfer Tax; details of their plans are not yet available, but it is safe to expect them to replace these two taxes with others.[39] Properly used, a system of taxation can encourage people to behave in some ways – acquire mortgages, save – and discourage others. The rapid changes in taxation of recent years give no confidence that intelligent decisions made now will come to fruition. This is no longer simply a middle-class problem. At present rates, a man earning only a half of the national average monthly manual wage pays income tax on each additional pound he earns. The insecurity created by rapid changes in policy is nearly universal.

The underlying conflict is between the instantaneous advantage to be gained from expedient political decisions and the slow maturation needed for any policy to be effective. This is not simply a conflict between the long run and the short run – though it certainly raises that problem – it also is a conflict between having a policy and making new policies. Local government housing schemes illustrate this point. In Scotland, at present, it takes an average of five years to build a council house.[40] Five years is not a long run. It is perhaps too long to build a council house. But when time to plan, acquire sites, obtain permission, acquire finance, obtain a builder and labour and then put up the bricks and mortar are all included five years is the average.

Knowing that the time-lapse is five years, a local authority might reasonably expect that four years from now it will be able to let the houses begun in the previous year and so on. But it is not so. In the *ten years* from 1964 to 1975 central-government circulars to local authorities ordered either the slowing-down or hurrying-up of house-building programmes (these speeds being one of the first regulators of the economy used by the Treasury) *nine times.* Five years is an average, but no one can, at any moment, count on it. Thus, a lack of a coherent sense of time in public affairs trips up the plans of government in many ways.

(5) *The lack of adequate knowledge*

The founders of the Labour Party were well aware that they did not know enough about the society in which they lived to be able to reform it successfully. If we do not know how many people are homeless, we cannot know how many homes to build. If we do not know how many schoolchildren there will be in ten years' time, we cannot know now how many classrooms to build or teachers to train. It was partly because they were aware of their ignorance, that they did not know the answers to questions like these, that Sidney and Beatrice Webb were moved to found the London School of Economics and Political Science and to start the *New Statesman*. The School was to encourage the discovery of the facts and the journal was to foster debate about how to use them. The Webbs were great optimists.

Despite the proliferation of departments of economics, social administration, political science, education, sociology, psychology and statistics in universities not only in Britain but throughout Europe and America, we still cannot give answers to many of the basic questions which social planners ask. Indeed, we now know that we probably will never have the kind of information required. Population forecasting is a notorious case in point. We need to know the number of people who will be living in Britain, and the number in the various age-groups, for all sorts of planning tasks. But population forecasts have consist-ently turned out to be wrong. The reason is not simply that forecasters have been using too few of the relevant variables. They have been confounded by trying to predict the behaviour of large numbers of people who change their minds. People decide that they want smaller families, or they decide, in large numbers, to postpone having a family until later in life. These changes of mind upset predictions, and without reasonably accurate predictions there can be no adequate planning. Those responsible have found it well-nigh impossible to estimate correctly the number of teacher-training places required – partly because they did not take the falling rate of births (after 1964) seriously enough soon enough – and partly because large numbers of women teachers decided all together that they would stay at their jobs for another few years rather than leave to start families. Sometimes planners are tripped up by their success. Our inner cities are now suffering from the too-successful attempts of previous generations of planners to move people out of the cities into new towns.

Our ignorance about society is such that a good many research reports end by stating that more research is needed if their small corner of society is to be understood. Often, too, research conclusions come up in the wrong form or at the wrong time for them to be of use. And yet even as we have too little knowledge, so, too, we have too much knowledge: there are so many surveys and reports, and so many administrators and politicians who need them, that they rarely connect at the right time.

All this is to say that our government is not organised, probably cannot be organised, so that knowledge and information flow from social scientists to governors and planners in the way the early members of the Labour Party may have hoped. But there are more sinister aspects to the relationship between those who have – or claim to have – expertise and ordinary citizens. Knowledge, or the pretence of having it, is a valuable resource in any political argument. The technologist or planner who knows, or thinks he knows, the benefits of demolishing a row of nineteenth-century housing and replacing it by new housing is in a position to dumbfound the less well-educated people who live in the old housing with science – or with what looks to them like science.

Sometimes the planners can also dominate the politicians. I attended a re-selection conference recently for a Labour councillor. At the meeting one local resident asked the councillor why she had voted against party policy and in favour of building a new road through the middle of her own ward. 'Because our officials, who carried out a survey, told us to' was the answer. Both the resident and the local councillor thought this was good enough. When Labour councillors and party workers give way to such arguments can it not be said that they are blinded by their own ideology? Their ideology teaches them that planning is a good thing and scientific planning a better one. Therefore they may feel, in some circumstances (for example, in relation to the decision to build a motorway through an old-established working-class district in central Edinburgh), that it is right to heed expert advice even when it is opposed to party policy.

There is a more general point here. Politics is about conflict, and socialists know this well. But science pretends to political neutrality. Experts may purport to have a vantage-point above the political fray from which to give unbiased advice. It cannot be denied that many people are ready to believe that experts do enjoy a vantage-point above the tumult and consequently to listen to them. The Labour Party's planning doctrine was, itself parasitic on this general respect for expert opinion. The party is therefore susceptible – like the Labour councillor whose readoption I observed – to the temptation to make a supine sacrifice of its own interests whenever these interests conflict with expert opinion.

It has recently become acceptable to oppose the ideas of the planners and to counterpose them to the wisdom of the people. Thinkers such as Norman Dennis have suggested that the proposals of planners should be checked by consulting the people affected by them. The Skeffington report, *People and Planning*, set out ways in which this could be done. Any contraposition of 'the people' with another group is one-sided. When it becomes possible to talk of 'the planners' as opposed to 'the people' we may be sure that the claims of the planners are out of favour. In itself the change is welcome. Nevertheless I think we must be wary of the new fashion, too. The notion that political decisions, such as whether a road should be built through a particular neighbourhood, can be decided by 'the people' begs the central issue: which people? This can be put another way: the notion that the people can all participate in decision-making satisfactorily is based on the same assumption as underlay Labour's planning doctrine – that is, on the assumption that there is some method of making political decisions which rise above the nasty conflict of human interests. There is not. 'Participation', with its implicit hope that all concerned will concur in the decisions made, is no more a way around this than was the idea of a centrally planned society run by technocratic socialist governments.

For all these reasons, the achievement of a planned society on the basis of the centralisation of resources in the hands of the state has raised problems unforeseen by Labour's ideologists in the 1930s. It should be said straight away that a number of these problems might well be alleviated by learning the lessons of the last twenty years. Most would seem less pressing if Britain were more prosperous; and, finally, there is no going back. Despite what Tory ideologists might say, the old world was, in many important respects, much worse than the present. We are talking here about the problems of affluence. In any case, the institutions and habits which supported the pre-Second World War society are destroyed. Even if one wanted to revive the *ancien régime*, the political support for the new practices is increasing and shows no sign of faltering. Governments of both parties now intervene in the economy and in Britons' lives in new ways with each passing year. The problems I have been enumerating are problems to deal with, not wish away.

The hopes which planned socialism gave rise to can now be seen to be naïve. At this stage, this doctrine in Labour's ideology must be rethought. The problems which moved Gaitskell and Crosland in the 1950s to doubt the wisdom of further nationalisation are now revealed to be much more deeply seated than they then realised. Neither is it the case that my arguments in this chapter apply only to those ideologists of the right. They apply with equal force against the planning socialism of the Left. Stuart Holland's recent *The Socialist Challenge* may be an angrier, a less temperate work, than Crosland's classic *Future of Socialism*, but its presumptions (if not the prescriptions) are similar. Holland, at one point, remarks: '. . . a major expansion of the public sector and a transformation of the at present unequally mixed economy would be necessary conditions for successful planning.'[41] Gaitskell and Crosland saw that the experience of 1945–51 drew a line between nationalisation and rational planning. The problems of the industries nationalised by the Attlee administration were too intractable to allow the new owners to use their industries to plan the economy. Gaitskell and Crosland thought planning required other tools and that promises of further nationalisation were irrelevant to the task of planning. They thus drew a line between future-oriented planning and old-fashioned past-oriented nationalisation schemes. As I have argued earlier, their distinction was overdrawn. They had forgotten the role that nationalisation still played in solidifying the ethos of the party.

I think we are now in a position to see that even their ideas still suffered from a hangover from the optimism of the 1930s. They did not see what is now manifest – planning is no panacea. It is not even a valuable socialist goal in itself.

IV

This setback is intellectually compelling: Planning is incredible. Perhaps one reason why participation has become such an attractive goal in recent years within the Labour movement is found here. Centralised control and participation are enemies. But the ideological cover for increasingly centralised control in the Labour movement was the doctrine of planning. Now that cover is wearing thin and the social, institutional and personal forces which have together won so many battles since the Second World War are dispersed.

When the Attlee government created the national health service one of the greatest battles within the Cabinet was between Bevan and Morrison. Morrison, the old warrior on behalf of local government in general and the London County Council in particular, hated to see his beloved municipally run hospitals taken over by the state and run centrally. Bevan argued for, and won, cabinet agreement for central control. One powerful argument in favour of central control was the need to plan so as to redistribute resources. Bevan's successors are busy travelling the land arguing the need for local control of health service provision.

Whether they will actually give up much authority to the provincial centres remains to be seen. We may be a bit sceptical: ministers do not like giving up authority, whatever their promptings of doctrine urge. But the newly fashionable demand for more local control is only powerful when combined with other forces. The Labour Party only became sympathetic to devolution to elect assemblies for Scotland and Wales after Scottish and Welsh voters in those previously Labour strongholds scared them by voting for the nationalist parties. The debate within the party on devolution was illustrative. It showed that only the old left was still committed to a centrally controlled and planned society. The party leaders and the unions opted for a discernible but as yet incoherent – and certainly brutal – doctrine which I called corporate socialism. This view is that the unity of the trade union and political wings is a sufficient condition of socialism: that what the Labour Party leadership and TUC leadership agree to is socialism. This doctrine, or proto-doctrine, is, of course, a corruption of one of the main themes in the ethos of the movement. Unity – solidarity, to give it its more militant name – is not a goal, it is a method. Shorn of a belief in any specific doctrine, the movement risks becoming a machine which wishes only for its own aggrandisement. One of the great ironies of this, I will argue in the next chapter, is that while all this has been going on Labour still has not thought out how it wants to use the machinery of state.

NOTES

1 Berki, R. N., *Socialism* (London, 1975), ch. 2.
2 Coates, K., *The Crisis of British Socialism* (Nottingham, 1972), p. 80.
3 *Economic Survey 1947*, cited in Bealey, F., *Social and Political Thought of the Labour Party* (London, 1970), p. 46.
4 Cripps, S., *Problems of a Socialist Government* (London, 1933).
5 Wise, E. F., in ibid., p. 69.
6 Mellor, in ibid., p. 114.
7 Cole, G. D. H., in ibid., p. 116.
8 Oldfield, A., 'The Labour Party and planning – 1934 or 1918', *Society for the Study of Labour History, Bulletin No. 25*, pp. 41–55.
9 ibid., p. 44.
10 Attlee, C., *The Labour Party in Perspective* (London, 1937).
11 Dalton, H., in Bealey, F., *Social and Political Thought*, pp. 142–3.
12 Webb, B. and S., in ibid., p. 172.
13 Brown, G., *Red Paper for Scotland* (Edinburgh, 1975), introduction.
14 Wootton, B., *Plan or No Plan* (London, 1934), p. 7.
15 Oldfield, 'Labour Party and planning', p. 55.
16 Lichtheim, G., *A Short History of Socialism* (London, 1970), p. 316.
17 Cited in Beer, S. H., *Modern British Politics: a Study of Parties and Pressure Groups* (London, 1965), p. 190.
18 Heclo, H. A. and Wildavsky, A., *The Private Government of Public Money* (London, 1974), ch. 8.

19   Skidelsky, R., *Politicians and the Slump: the Labour Government of 1929–31* (London, 1967).
20   Oldfield, 'Labour Party and planning', p. 42.
21   Quoted in Beer, *Modern British Politics*, p. 192.
22   See also Brittan, S., *Steering the Economy: The Role of the Treasury* (Harmondsworth, 1971), pp. 182ff.
23   Quoted in Beer, *Modern British Politics*, p. 194.
24   ibid., p. 201.
25   ibid., p. 191, and Brittan, *Steering the Economy*.
26   See Klein, R., *Inflation and Priorities* (London, 1975), pp. 1–2.
27   Durbin, E., *The Politics of Democratic Socialism* (London, 1940), p. 96.
28   Lichtheim, *Socialism*, p. 315.
29   See David McKie in the *Guardian*, 13 February 1975, p. 15.
30   Klein, *Inflation and Priorities*, p. 8. See also *Which?*, August 1975.
31   Owen, D., in *Sunday Times*, 12 October 1975, p. 6.
32   Klein, *Inflation and Priorities*, pp. 92–5.
33   ibid., pp. 92–5.
34   ibid., pp. 88–91.
35   See Raison, R., and Connelly, Naomi, 'Law and order', in Klein, *Inflation and Priorities*, pp. 175–93; Owen, D., in the *Sunday Times*, 12 October 1975, p. 6.
36   Gregory, R., cited in Rose, R., 'Overloaded governments?', unpublished paper, 1975.
37   King, A., 'Overload: problems of governing in the 1970s', *Political Studies*, vol. 23, 1975, p. 291.
38   Jackson, D., *et al.*, *Do Trade Unions Cause Inflation?* (Cambridge, 1975), pp. 48–50.
39   Stanley, O., 'Runaway politics of inflation', *The Times*, 6 October 1975.
40   Cook, R., in Brown, *Red Paper for Scotland*, p. 342.
41   Holland, S., *The Socialist Challenge* (London, 1975), p. 223.

5
Socialist Ministers:
An Ideological Dilemma

I

A democratic Socialist movement that attempts to transform a capitalist into a socialist order is necessarily faced with a choice between two incompatibles – principles and power.[1]

This was Peter Gay's verdict on the career of Edward Bernstein and the pre-First World War German Social Democratic Party in which Bernstein was a leading theorist. It is a curious fact of history that the two most powerful and frequently cited critiques of social democracy, Gay's *The Dilemma of Democratic Socialism* and Robert Michels' *Political Parties*, are both about the German SPD in the period before it was elected to office.

The first Social Democratic Party in a major country to gain office with a majority in its Parliament based on a near-majority (48 per cent) of popular votes was the British Labour Party. Its victory occurred in 1945. It is not obvious that studies of a party *before* it has won office can tell us much about how it will behave *in* or *after* it has office. This difficulty did not trouble either Michels or Gay, or those who extrapolited from their studies of the SPD to all social democratic parties, because they believed that the experience of the party before it gained office was decisive. In short, both Michels and Gay agreed that social democracy was inherently futile. Nevertheless, these classic studies of the SPD are a useful beginning-point for a study of how office has affected the ideology of the Labour Party.

Michels' critique of social democracy focused, as its sub-title promised, on 'the oligarchical tendencies of modern democracy'. It was a sociological study of the German Social Democratic Party machine which brought to the reader's attention the way the party machine acquired a momentum of its own and increasingly diverged from the ideals which had inspired its formation. These divergences

were widened by the conflict between the proletarian need for a
revolutionary political party, on the one hand, and the desire of the
party's full-time officials for a secure trouble-free career with a
pension at the end of it, on the other.[2] Michels's analysis suggested
that whether or not such a social democratic party gained power was
irrelevant since the party would long since have lost the will or ability
to bring about socialism even if it held the formal reins of state power.
Gay emphasised the electoral, as opposed to the organisational,
problems of social democracy. As he put it:

There are two reasons why democratic mass parties tend to slough
off any revolutionary vigor they may have possessed. Not that a
large party necessarily loses 'class purity'. . . . German Social
Democracy remains surprisingly proletarian. But, in the first place,
considerable segments of the proletarian party members are in-
different or even hostile to revolution. This hostility has a variety
of causes: fear, complacency, devotion to authority and legality.
And secondly, a mass party must think of more than its membership.
It has followers who endorse its programme and vote for its
candidates but do not belong to it. This imposes upon the party the
need for flexibility designed to attract even larger numbers of votes.
Once a Socialist party enters into the vote-catching game, that
magic figure, 51 per cent, tends to obscure other considerations.[3]

On this analysis the dilemma of social democracy is complete and its
failure to achieve socialism guaranteed: it cannot both remain true to
its ideals and gain office through election. And it may, Gay should
have added, do neither.

Since both of these analyses were primarily about the experience
of the SPD before it gained office they were safe from any potentially
embarrassing attempt to check their prognostications against the
performance. There was then no record of social democratic government to examine. This is no longer the case. But subsequent experience
in Germany tends to confirm the Gay thesis. The German SPD has
now a very creditable record as a party of government behind it.
However, in postwar Germany it only achieved office after formally
abandoning its attempt to destroy capitalism.

In Britain, however, the record of Labour governments does not
immediately seem either to confirm or to deny either the Michels or
Gay thesis. This record, I want to argue, suggests that social democrats
in office have indeed faced dilemmas – dilemmas different from those
faced by their Conservative opponents – but that they are different in
kind from those predicted by Gay.

If we look at the record of the three Labour majority governments
(1945–51, 1964–70 and 1974–   ) we see that problems have arisen

not so much from too much theory or from theory betrayed but from too little theory. The Labour Party's ideology does not contain a sufficiently coherent theory of the state or of our politics. It has a theory about elections and has adopted – with very little change – the radical liberal view of the constitution and of the respective roles of elections, party, Parliament and government contained in that view.

What it has signally failed to do is to argue out what is meant by 'achieving socialism', and hence it has no guide for its representatives once they are in office. The really frustrating dilemma of democratic socialism arises not merely, as Gay suggests, from its need to attract electoral support from the non-socialist majority of the electorate, but also from its ministers' lack of a theoretical vocabulary in which satisfactorily to pursue their socialism and to explain their actions in this pursuit to their own activists.

This lack of political vocabulary is a feature of the Labour Party which it shares with many other socialist parties. The experience of socialist government in the Soviet Union provides, of course, the obvious material for a socialist theory of politics, but the disadvantages of that system have been so often trumpeted by its enemies that even its friends are now ashamed to learn any lessons from it. What one encounters in the political writings of socialists, in and beyond the Labour Party, is a critique of politics in a capitalist society. C. Wright Mills's *The Power Elite* is a good example; Ralph Miliband's *The State in Capitalist Society* is an application of Mills's ideas to contemporary Britain. Such critiques are an important step but they stop short at the crucial point. They fail to distinguish between the features of government in a capitalist society and the features of government as such.

The features of government which occur in socialist societies – extensive bureaucracy, lack of accountability of rulers to ruled, politicisation of previously private realms, one-party states – could be seriously examined to distinguish between those which are echoes of the past which may in time disappear, and those which are inescapable features of technologically sophisticated, economically advanced, large societies. Does anyone believe that any such state will ever do without a bureaucracy? But Labour's leaders lack any political theory in their background.

II

In place of a theory of politics – of, that is to say, any coherent idea of how the government works and how they propose to use it – the Labour Party has what one commentator has misleadingly called a 'theory of the mandate'.[4] It is not really a theory; let us call it 'manifestoism'. Manifestoism is the Labour Party's adaptation of the nineteenth-century radical theory of politics to the ethos of the working class.

Describing this ideology abstractly it looks like this. The party nominates parliamentary candidates; these candidates commit themselves, if elected to Parliament, to 'carry out the provisions of the manifesto'; a manifesto is written for each election by the NEC; it is the collective duty of Labour's elected representatives to criticise government actions on the basic of the manifesto when Labour is out of office and to enact it when in office. All shades of opinion within the parliamentary party argue that their position is nearest to the meaning of the manifesto. This is true of both the Tribune Group and the recently formed Manifesto Group.

This ideology revolves around the assumption of the sovereignty within the party of the annual conference. Manifestoism is an attempt to control an executive – a Labour Cabinet, for example – and make it responsive to the ideas and wishes of the party. It fits neatly into the radical theory of the constitution which emphasises the sovereignty of Parliament and grounds that sovereignty on democratic election. It is about representation first of all and only secondarily, and indirectly, about governing.

Manifestoism makes no concession of principle to the parts of the British constitution which emphasise the right of the Cabinet to co-ordinate policy, or to adjust to changing circumstances, or to the possibility that the political world is different in any important respect from how it appears to the majority of delegates at party conferences. It is an outsiders' ideology – a populist ideology – and one which is intolerant of any Labour representative who does not acknowledge its claims.

In practice, of course, the details of manifestos are so badly worked out that a Labour Cabinet can often present its actions – whatever they may be – as consistent with the manifesto. Manifestos consist of lists of policies for action. Typically, as in the case of the manifesto for the October 1974 election, they begin with a description of the major tasks which the party thinks it will confront if elected. They then go on to describe how the party proposes to tackle these tasks. These policies are occasionally contradictory, frequently vague, rarely put in any order of priority (despite what may be said to the contrary) and almost never tied to any specific timetable. Above and beyond these difficulties it is also the case that the constitution of the Labour Party is itself vague and even, in places, contradictory about the roles to be assigned to the various organs of the party in implementing the constitution. This vagueness is no more than is to be expected of a party which is part of a larger movement which, by definition, has no precise chain of command. But the fact remains that manifestoism is widespread in the party and that it leads to a general expectation of fulfilment by the Parliamentary Labour Party. These expectations are, naturally, at their highest when Labour is in office.

The Labour Party has succeeded, to no small extent, in getting manifestoism accepted as part of political life in Britain. The Labour Party was, for a long time, the national party which made most of regularly issuing a manifesto. The Liberals and Conservatives followed suit, but have never invested the manifesto with the same authority. Traditionally, in the Tory Party, the party's election manifesto was the leader's speech to the annual conference preceding the election. The manifesto was seen to be the embodiment of the ideas of the leader, and hence his to change as he saw fit. The first manifesto on the lines of the Labour Party's creations came from the Tory Party in time for the 1950 election – i.e. for the first election after their first defeat by a majority Labour Party. It was called *This Is the Road*.[5] In general, the Conservative and Liberal parties retain some distance from socialist ideas about manifestoism. For the older parties victory in an election is generally treated as 'a mandate to govern' as best they can. In any case, in the Tory Party, the committees which draft the manifesto are all directly responsible to (and, indeed, appointed by) the leader, so that the 'democratic' authority which a manifesto has in the Labour Party is absent in the case of the Tory Party.

Manifestoism is not a theory of politics, but an attempt to control Labour's barely trusted elected leaders. If it were a theory (or part of a theory), there would be a much better worked-out conception of how the manifesto was to be implemented. It would also require some method of enforcing accountability to the annual conference. We have seen in recent years how badly lacking such a procedure is, and what a high price the party pays for it.

One current focus of confusion in the party concerns the question of who is responsible for disciplining Labour MPs and on what grounds. Is an MP responsible to the National Executive Committee, who are charged with interpreting the resolutions of the annual conference and writing the manifesto; or is he responsible to his constituency party, who in fact selected him as the party's candidate and who can decide whether or not to readopt him; or to the annual conference; or to the Party Whip, who can deny him membership of the parliamentary party; or to the leader, who can deny him prefer-ment; or is he responsible to some combination of these groups? What will not do, once the question is asked, is for him not to know from one moment to another to whom he is responsible. And yet that is the position. Because the party has no real theory of politics it has no way of deciding such questions.

In practice this complexity may do little immediate harm. The party, on all levels, operates its incoherent constitutions by simply being very tolerant .When one looks at those cases of MPs who have had a hard time from their constituency parties in recent years – and they are few – it is difficult to be very sympathetic to the MPs. A Labour MP, like Reg Prentice, who refuses to meet a delegation of trade unionists on a matter which is important to them is so stiff-necked and insensitive as to deserve any trouble he gets from his constituency party (a point Mr Prentice confirmed when he quit Labour for the Conservative Party). This kind of trouble can be avoided so easily in practice that it hardly seems necessary to invent a theory of politics to resolve it. But the Tory Party rarely has this kind of trouble, and the Labour Party suffers it a few times each Parliament; the cumulative effect is to make many people in the party edgy and show the advantage of a better-defined relationship. The problems which a few stiff-necked MPs have with troublesome constituency parties serves, I think, to show in a rather minor, even trivial, way the difficulties which the whole movement is increasingly encountering.

There have now been three periods of majority Labour government. The speculations of Gay and Michels are no longer adequate. We have seen actual Labour governments struggle under this notion of manifestoism and, increasingly, the thinness of the ideology is becoming apparent. For a time it was possible to believe that the failure of this or that minister to implement his bit of manifesto was the result of particular circumstances operating in his case. How long can this belief continue? Perhaps the strongest reaction within the party to the failures of the 1964–70 government was an enhanced literal attachment to subsequent manifestos. Is this not just a hopeless attempt to hold on to a myth which is half-realised to be unavailing?

Up to a point, manifestoism contains a mechanism which protects the ideology against any blame which may attach to its not being fulfilled. It places all the blame for the failure on the minister or Ministry concerned. The Minister is said to have betrayed the movement. This accusation is reinforced in a crucial respect by all the hopes and fears which are built into the feeling of class-consciousness. The workers send representatives to Parliament to defend their interests. The very act of going to Parliament, of living the life of an MP with a middle-class salary, a secretary and all the other accoutrements of parliamentary life means that the MP lives in a middle-class world in a middle-class way. Hence the very business of being elected to represent working-class interests takes an MP out of the world he is meant to represent and into the camp of the enemy. Hence election opens him to the charge of having betrayed these interests. Michels's book gains plausibility from, and owes much of its popularity to, the fact that Michels (a disenchanted socialist activist) describes this change from the point of view of the socialist activist. He speaks in the idiom of this activist and awakens the fears born of defensiveness which are so powerful in the activist's ethos. People who believe in an ideology strongly enough to spend many hours in the necessary but repetitive work of running a local party can be very suspicious of those who profit from their work.[6]

A party which, on the one hand, wants to remain true to an ethos of oppression and, on the other hand, wants to build a parliamentary government imposes intolerable demands on its representatives. They are placed in a dilemma by the inability of manifestoism to explain to them or their supporters how they should rule. Until now this dilemma of Labour's representatives has been obscured from its activists by use of the slippery and ambiguous categories of class. Every time a leader slipped or had to make a decision which was not anticipated by the manifesto, he could then be denounced as a class traitor. The movement, having thus explained the deviation from the pure path of the manifesto to its own satisfaction, could continue on its own way untroubled. The dream that the parliamentary party could somehow achieve socialism could thus be preserved in the face of repeated failures.

Ramsay MacDonald, Labour's first Prime Minister is, of course, the arch-dupe in this charade. In 1924 and again in 1929 and 1931 he became Prime Minister, a job which broke him. His reputation has had to pay the price for his undoubted inadequacies many times over. He provides a convenient scapegoat for the failure of the Labour Party from 1906 to 1945. No party based on manifestoism was going to achieve socialism in that or any other period. A party that does not know what it wants, or how it proposes to get it, or why it holds the particular weapons to achieve its ends that it does hold, can be sure of one thing – it won't get it.

Manifestoism protects the constituency activists – the brave authors of resolutions without end – from having to accept any responsibility for the acts of their leaders. Hence, MacDonald and his like can be disowned. This failure makes life easier for some of Labour's leaders. They, too, can escape responsibility for the acts of government. This luxury is allowed them when they lead the Opposition. Thus, it is not surprising that we have in the Parliamentary Labour Party the last great defenders of parliamentary democracy. No other system offers such a prominent role to those who merely criticise and attack. If parliamentary forms were ever totally discredited in Britain – and replaced by a combination of referenda and multi-lateral interest-group bargaining – the Labour Party would be the greatest loser. The arguments heard from within the Labour Party during the 1975 referendum on British membership of the Common Market more than gave the game away. The party supposedly dedicated to achieving socialism and abolishing capitalism split on Common

Market membership. The majority of the party in Parliament and at a special party conference were opposed to membership. The argument against membership of the Community most frequently heard from that majority centred on their desire to protect parliamentary sovereignty. A fine concern for a socialist! Why did the Labour anti-Europeans want to protect parliamentary sovereignty? Because they believed it provided especially effective devices of opposition. To this, very large, section of the party the most comfortable place to be is on the Opposition front bench. There, in Parliament, in opposition, they can feel that they have power and yet need take responsibility only for making speeches.

It is hardly an accident that the hero of this, the majority and the heart of the movement, is Aneurin Bevan. Bevan's greatest achievement, perhaps the one transcendent act of the Labour Party, was the creation of the national health service. This creation could, of course, only be accomplished by a party of government, not a mere opposition. And yet this achievement, for which, incidentally, manifestoism is hard put to take credit since the idea of the national health service came from the Beveridge Report (a non-partisan matter) and Bevan himself pushed the new service further than the 1945 manifesto commanded, seems not to have been Bevan's happiest hour.

It is still possible to read Michael Foot's biography of his mentor and believe that Bevan's happiest role was as a leading figure in the Opposition during the wartime coalition from 1940–5. There, free from the compromises (in office he was forced to allow some national health hospital beds to be available to those who could pay for them, and within the party he was forced to abandon his left-wing unilateral disarmament friends when he asked them not to send him, a potential Labour Foreign Minister 'naked into the Conference Chamber') of government or party leadership he could attack on any ground that suited him and yet never have to carry the can.

In this role Bevan reached the highest peak that a Labour representative can rise to without having to face the dilemma of power. This is the role often eulogised in the radical liberal tradition; it is leadership understood as tribune of the people. Michael Foot's preference for this role even outside of its use in the Labour Party is clear in his early book, *The Pen and the Sword*.[7] 'The Pen' is Foot's hero Jonathan Swift, and 'The Sword' his great adversary Marlborough. The book is an account of the struggle between Foot and Bevan's spiritual ancestor, Swift, and Churchill's biological ancestor. Swift, the journalist who had ministers in daily fear of the acid of his pen, is an attractive emblem of one of the wings of the Labour Party. I do not wish to minimise the historical importance of that role. Few things in public life are as important or noble as the defence of the weak, but is this role sufficient for a ruling class?

III

If leadership of the parliamentary opposition is a refuge from the dilemma of democratic socialism, there is no escape for Labour's ministers. They are the leaders of the led, and manifestoism is of precious little help to them in this role.

In the nineteenth century the British constitution evolved two different roles for senior politicians: executive and opposition. I have suggested that manifestoism, based on radical liberalism, has driven Labour leaders to be more at home in the second role. But the Constitution allows no separation; to play one role one must be convincing in the other. The leaders of the Opposition are an alternative government. The Constitution presumes further that effective opposition is only possible for leaders who demonstrate (not least to themselves) that they are capable of taking over the executive immediately. In theory a party in opposition prepares itself to take the executive position. As Roy Jenkins put it: 'The best test of an Opposition is the extent to which it uses a period of pause to prepare for office.'[8]

To an outsider the extraordinary thing about this facet of the constitution, both in theory and practice, is the way roles are switched overnight. In fact, the Labour Party has had rather more trouble changing from opposition to ministry than the theory suggests it ought. If we look at the published memoirs and biographies of Labour ministers and ex-ministers we see that they have handled this role-change in two different and equally unsatisfactory ways.

There is, first of all, the reaction which one notices in Herbert Morrison, Patrick Gordon Walker and, though to a lesser extent, in Roy Jenkins and Anthony Crosland. They become so drawn into the playing of the Whitehall game as, almost, to forget what it is for. Morrison and Patrick Gordon Walker have published detailed, almost loving, certainly uncritical, accounts of how the machine operates. Gordon Walker observes:

> In practice there has been a certain growing together of Cabinet and Civil Service. The tendency, as old as the Cabinet itself, for a Minister to identify himself with the continuing policy of his department becomes stronger.[9]

It would be wrong to suggest that he speaks only for himself. According to Bruce Headey's study of Cabinet ministers, Gordon Walker's attitude is characteristic of ministers both Labour and Conservative. Headey could find only a tiny (6 per cent) proportion of ministers or ex-ministers who thought it was their duty to 'implement party policy or to take decisions in accordance with party policy'. [10]

Those who do not accept this manifestoist role (the other 94 per cent) leave themselves wide open to the charge – indeed, they admit the force of the charge – that they have abandoned the manifesto. They can be defended by two related arguments. First on grounds of coherence. The party spends much of its time and energy electing governments. It cannot complain if its ministers then govern. To deny these ministers this right would require reopening the entire question of whether a socialist movement has any business forming a political party to contest parliamentary seats in the first place. Since the party is unwilling to reopen that question, or to forbid MPs to accept ministerial office (as the SPD once did), it can hardly complain if they play the games for which the party has placed them.

Again, and much more seriously, Labour's ministers can claim that, whatever the particular manifestos of the party say on the matter, in government they can ease the way for those they represent in a myriad of ways. They can use the state apparatus to legitimise and further the aspirations and material interests of their voters. They can even execute.

Because many of the actions of the government – certainly the overwhelming majority of its decisions – are day-to-day executive decisions affecting individual citizens or small groups of people, it is not even possible for the manifesto to concern itself with these decisions except in an exhortatory way: 'We shall continue to work for a peaceful and just settlement of the disputes in the Middle East and Cyprus in the light of the declarations of the United Nations and our own responsibilities, as the October 1974 manifesto said.[11] This is particularly true of decisions taken at a low level in the Home Office – whether or not to review a particular prisoner's request for parole – and, on a lower level, in the Department of Health and Social Security – how to interpret a particular family's need for supplementay benefit.

It is also increasingly the case that major changes in policy, such as the decision to establish comprehensive schools, can only be made with the assent of the powerful groups affected. In the case of education, as well as any other activity controlled by a profession, or a trade union, or entrepreneurs, or local government, the national government can get what it wants only by the consent of the groups involved. Anthony Crosland always felt very acutely the need to win over the teachers' groups to the concept of comprehensive schooling and did his best to lessen the ire of the local authorities who would have to implement his plans.[12] He was careful to act so as to encourage these groups to co-operate with him where their opposition could have wrecked his plans and soured any other hopes he may have had. The manifesto can demand comprehensive schools but it takes the skill of the minister, not a demand or command from anyone, to carry out the policy. Hence, even though Labour's ministers may become too wrapped up in their new roles, there is good reason for them to move beyond the remit of the party manifesto.

Crosland's actions while at the Department of Education and Science could, I am sure, be successfully defended as consistent with the manifesto. It promised change; he produced changes. But there is a danger to a position like this which comes from the absurdly literalist and mechanical interpretation of ministerial powers which manifestoism can inspire. The Labour movement is full of splendid rhetoric about 'making these levers work for us' and hopes of taking 'the commanding heights of the economy'. Shawcross's cry, 'We are the masters now', was resonant in the hearts of Labour's supporters to the extent that these supporters shared this hope. Such phrases are believed within the movement. It is a matter of repeated, sad, observation to me that year after year people join constituency parties because they think that there are levers 'up there' in government which they, in a small way, can help pull. When Labour's MPs become ministers and nothing drastic happens such expectations are disappointed. A measure of the degree of disappointment can be taken from the declining individual membership of the party. During the 1964–70 government membership fell dramatically. It has never recovered. In 1964 individual membership totalled 830,116; by 1970 one member in six had left – the total was down to 680,191. One reason for such a fall during a Labour government was the exaggerated hopes which brought people in, in the first place. Social democrat ministers are attacked from within the party by these disappointed people as a result of the way the ministers fulfil its promises.

If the first reaction to the social democratic dilemma involves the danger that the minister (or government) will become estranged from the movement, the opposite reaction of Barbara Castle and Richard Crossman also has its dangers. Castle and Crossman never trusted themselves or Whitehall sufficiently and so were unable to use the machine effectively. Both remained deeply suspicious of their role as ministers and both resisted its claims on them. Castle reported almost exactly the opposite of Gordon Walker's reaction:

. . . what politicians do not take on board until they become Ministers is the extent to which from the moment a Minister walks out of that Cabinet room at No. 10 Downing Street having been asked by the Prime Minister to take on such and such a job, the Civil Service takes over his life.[13]

Crossman begins his memoirs with a nearly identical observation:

. . . and already I realise the tremendous effort it requires not to be taken over by the Civil Service. My Minister's room is like a padded cell, and in certain ways I am like a person who is suddenly certified a lunatic and put safely into this great vast room, cut off from real life and surrounded by male and female trained nurses and attendants.[14]

Here we see a very different reaction from that of Morrison, Gordon Walker and Jenkins.

Castle and Crossman's reaction is to take the other horn of this dilemma of democratic socialism. They remain acutely conscious of what their people want and of how foreign the cliques in Whitehall are to their constituency workers, but at the price of making very ineffective use of their position as ministers. It is in evaluating their use of civil servants that one feels most keenly the lack of any socialist political theory. A socialist minister has to avoid two traps: he has to avoid becoming a tool of the Whitehall clique, and he has to avoid so alienating that clique that he cannot use them to execute his policy and run his ministry. Both these traps are set for Conservatives as well – a good number of them have fallen into one or other – but at least Conservatives do not come to office predisposed to be opposition-minded. They have other problems. Opposition-mindedness on the part of ministers blinds them to the difference between opposition to the ministerial view (which is the right and proper business of any socialist) and opposition to the ministry. Crossman and Castle made full assaults on their ministries as such. In strikingly similar language, both have written of their encasement within their ministries.

Crossman and Castle make little attempt to disguise their hostility towards their senior civil servants. It is here, in the relationship between the more literally manifestoist Labour ministers and their senior civil servants – especially their private offices – that the dilemma is seen at its starkest. Effective government, effective use of the Whitehall machine, depends very centrally on the ability of ministers and civil servants to do their different jobs together. Crosland recognised this, as his answer to a question from Maurice Kogan shows:

Kogan: May we now turn to relations with civil servants? Is the popular assumption about bureaucratic obstructionism a fair one?

Crosland: No, certainly not. It's very rare that you meet real resistance or obstruction. I can think of only a few instances [he names two but says he got his way both times].[15]

Later he added:

Crosland: But generally I never found any problem in establishing good working relations. And a Minister who doesn't do so is wasting a large fund of knowledge and expertise.[16]

Harold Wilson, who was himself a civil servant during the Second World War, gave a similar answer to a similar question from Norman Hunt:

Wilson: The idea of some people that a change of government means sabotage from the Civil Service is, I think, nonsense.[17]

and

Wilson: My problem was I was getting too much information and too much work . . . [at the Board of Trade in the 1945 government].[18]

This is a view which Wilson substantially endorsed after resigning as Prime Minister in 1976. In his *The Governance of Britain* he endorses the establishment view of the impartiality of civil servants particularly when dealing with a recently elected administration. He reports that, on arriving at his new ministry, each new minister

. . . is welcomed, briefed and handed a mass of documentation for reading himself in.
     The Civil Service is extremely agile and politically, almost cynically, dispassionate in reading the electoral portents. Not only does the Cabinet Office, during this election period prepare two alternative Queen's speeches reflecting the respective parties' election manifestos; each department of state is preparing the necessary policy guidance on the main issues affecting departmental work.[19]

Whatever may have been the case in the relatively simple political world in which the Labour Party was born and acquired its notions of the constitution, the processes of government are now so complicated that a minister who tries – as Crossman obviously did – to ignore or bypass his civil servants is not going to be very effective. Roy Jenkins, with his customary equanimity, makes the point:

This does not mean, except in exceptional circumstances, that a Minister has to batter his head against a brick wall of determined opposition. If he knows what he wants to do he will not in general have much difficulty in getting his policy carried out. . . . Equally, unless he is incredibly rash and pigheaded, he is bound to be deflected by the right of argument from certain courses to which he was originally attached.[20]

Castle and Crossman did not see it that way. Symptomatic of their view was their complaint of being cosseted by their civil servants and denied any chance to speak to people outside the official net. Castle claims that she had to 'lie like a trooper' about her timetable to have an informal meeting with her constituency secretary. Crossman, who preferred other company, records the angry reaction he incurred when he consulted friends outside the ministry. Both ministers were appalled by the system of official committees (PESC mainly) which they thought their own civil servants were using to sabotage their plans.

In both cases it is clear that the distrust was returned measure for measure. Crossman makes no bones about his trouble with his Permanent Secretary, Dame Evelyn Sharpe, and he well knew she reciprocated his feelings. Barbara Castle's remarks make clear just how difficult to deal with she was. Bruce Headey reports severe criticism of her work which he heard when doing his research. One civil servant told Headey that Castle had 'a big bill mentality' – that wherever she went she felt compelled to make her mark by passing a large reform Bill which embodied important parts of the manifesto. Headey's source (anonymous, of course) complained that Castle was so intent on having something to show that she was often heedless of the long-term consequences of her Bill. We see in that remark a sign of the tension which exists between the civil servants – who actually do the vast majority of the administration – and ministers of any party. Harold Macmillan met such resistance when he was responsible for speeding up the rate of house-building.

But the problems of Labour ministers are increased by the suspicion of their supporters that unless they are seen to be having trouble with their civil servants they cannot be doing their job properly (it is noticeable that – in self-defence? – a sizeable number of Labour ministers have written books on the constitution and on their relations with their civil servants). If they satisfy their supporters' expectations, they have trouble using the machine effectively; if they use the machine effectively, they are suspected of betraying the movement. But they are sent to Whitehall to use it for the movement.

On one level the choice between the horns of the dilemma may be just a matter of style. It is certainly not a matter of being 'right' or 'left'. Mr Prentice was universally identified as a right-winger, yet his period in the Department of Education was characterised – marred, I have heard teachers say – by a literal devotion to carrying out the manifesto. When his constituency party decided not to readopt him, his own refusal to acknowledge their claims on him – his style – was an obvious factor. Mr Jenkins, on the other hand, a man also associated with the right, has written convincingly and attractively of the life of a minister, making no attempt to hide the fact that he found great satisfaction in 'doing something worth while'.[21] At one point in his *Diaries*, Crossman reflects despairingly on Harold Wilson's love of going off and having a few pints of beer with his constituency workers. Not for Crossman the beery matiness of working-class conviviality.[22] His commitment to the manifesto and to socialism was the literal commitment of an intellectual to an ideal.

IV

Part of the friction between Labour ministers and their civil servants arises from the differences between the organisations which support them. The entire ideology of the civil service, like that of broadcasting and scholarship, emphasises its neutrality and objectivity. A civil servant is meant to execute the policies of a Labour government one day and those of a Tory government the next, and pursue the goals of each in turn with equal skill. The constitutional doctrines of ministerial responsibility in which every government maintains the fiction that each minister knows, and is responsible for, all the actions of his ministry; and of collective responsibility of the government in which the ministers agree to defend all Cabinet policies in public including ones they patently know nothing about – both hinge on the policylessness of the civil service.

As Jeremy Bray (also an ex-Labour minister) has pointed out, there is something ridiculous and faintly incredible about the role assigned to the civil service in both these doctrines. On the one hand, the civil service are thought to have sufficient wisdom and insight to be very privileged advisers; on the other, they are expected to be doormats accepting each and every policy of successive governments and allowing all credit for them to their political masters.

The ideology of objectivity tries to make this paradox palatable. The other side of this ideology is less defensive. It points to the civil service ethos of efficiency and expeditiousness: civil servants get things done – and woe to any minister who thinks he can fix things behind their backs. The Labour Party has never taken this point to heart. Its evidence to the Fulton Committee (interestingly, the Conservative Party submitted no evidence) urged the creation of a series of political *cabinets*, on the French model, to allow ministers to have alternative sources of information and advice.[23] Governments of both parties have experimented in limited ways with ideas of this kind since the Fulton Report. Labour ministers, in particular, have tried to supplement the departmental views of their civil servants with political advice from their own 'political' advisers. It is much too early to evaluate the success of this experiment (it will be difficult to evaluate it because each case seems to be unique), but the experience of political advisers during the 1964–70 government was that the civil service could freeze them out. They can be rendered ineffective by being denied information, or by being given too much information, or by being given it too late.[24]

Most party members (as opposed to ministers) have never quite accepted that a group of people can effectively help them even though they are not appointed by and responsible to the party. Any minister who makes it clear that he disagrees is liable to the charge of betraying his class. In this respect, the party's ethos is the reverse of that of the civil service. The Labour Party emphasises the doctrinal part of its ideology and is barely conscious of its ethos. In addition its ethos is distinctively working class. It emphasises loyalty and steadfastness. The civil service, on the other hand, has a very strong ethos of which it is intensely proud. It is an ethos for which an education in an English public school is an excellent preparation. It emphasises wit, versatility and agility. At the same time the ideology of the civil service requires that the service have no doctrines whatever. Indeed, it is consonant with that strain of the British middle-class ethos which is proud of its doctrinelessness. One might, at first glance, expect these two ideologies to complement each other: the party could provide the doctrines and the civil service execute the policies which arise out of them. But it does not work like that. Neither side likes the smell of the other. This leads to suspicion.

This particular suspicion is the source of the present dilemma of democratic socialism. Like the dilemma observed by Gay, it is the product of a particular historical situation. In time it may be overcome or it may be the undoing of the party: the former will occur if the party and the movement learn to live with power and not fear it; the latter will occur if the defensiveness of the movement is too strong to be overcome and it retreats in disgust from the responsibilities and disappointments which power brings.

NOTES

1   Gay, P., *The Dilemma of Democratic Socialism: Edward Bernstein's Challenge to Marx* (New York, 1952), p. ix.
2   Michels, R., *Political Parties: A Sociological Study of the Oligarchic Tendencies of Modern Democrary* (New York, 1959).
3   Gay, P., *Democratic Socialism*, p. 102.
4   Birch, A. H., *Representative and Responsible Government* (London, 1969), pp. 116ff. The notion that Labour's voters know what is in the manifesto or actually vote for it has been usefully punctured by Richard Rose. Rose has an impressive track-record at puncturing such myths. See Rose, R., *Politics in England Today* (London, 1974).
5   Cited in McKenzie, R. T., *British Political Parties: The Distribution of Power within the Conservative and Labour Parties*, 2nd edn (London, 1963).

6 These suspicions are, I do not wish to deny, often well founded.
7 Foot, M., *The Pen and the Sword: A Year in the Life of Jonathan Swift* (London, 1966).
8 Jenkins, R., 'In and out of power', *Observer*, 20 June 1971, p. 9.
9 Walker, P. Gordon, *The Cabinet*, revised edn (London, 1972), p. 66.
10 Headey, B., *British Cabinet Ministers: The Roles of Politicians in Executive Office* (London, 1974), p. 61. He adds: 'It would be hard to imagine that thirty or forty years ago Labour leaders in particular would have omitted to mention as one of their main roles the implementation of party principles.'
11 *The Labour Party Manifesto, October 1974*, p. 27.
12 Kogan, M., *The Politics of Education* (Harmondsworth, 1971).
13 Castle, B., 'Mandarin power', *Sunday Times*, 10 June 1973, p. 17.
14 Crossman, R. H. S., *The Diaries of a Cabinet Minister*, Vol. 1, *Minister of Housing 1964–66* (London, 1975), p. 21.
15 Kogan, *Politics of Education*, p. 176.
16 ibid., p. 182.
17 Hunt, N., *Whitehall and Beyond* (London, 1964), p. 11.
18 ibid., p. 22.
19 Wilson, H., *The Governance of Britain* (London, 1976), p. 42.
20 Jenkins, R., 'The reality of political power', *Sunday Times*, 17 January 1971, pp. 25–6.
21 Jenkins, R., 'In and out of power'.
22 Crossman, *Diaries*, Vol. I, p. 172.
23 Bray, J., *Decision in Government* (London, 1970), p. 64.
24 See Hudson, M., 'Political secretaries', *Political Quarterly*, vol. 43, no. 43, July–September 1976.

6
Our Rulers' Natural Party?

It is too easy to conceive of the difference between doctrine and ethos in the Labour Party as the difference between the ideology of the party as it affects the party's leaders and as it affects its supporters; or, to be more precise, the ideology of the party as it informs, on the one hand, the parliamentary party and, on the other hand, the general management committees (GMCs) of the constituency parties. For most of the history of the party this distinction could not be made to stick. In the 1930s, after the 1931 election, the parliamentary party was too small, and too discredited by the betrayal of 1931, to dominate the party. All sections of the party were stronger in the country than in Parliament. Certainly, in the period between the 1931 general election and the formation of the wartime coalition in 1940 both the ethos or, if one likes, the heart of the party and its doctrinal head were alive in the GMCs. It was at this time that the doctrinal ideas of the Communist Party, as mediated through organisations such as the Left Book Club and the attempts at a Popular Front against Fascism, came to have their greatest influence in the GMCs. The parliamentary party did its best to tag along with the ideas then bubbling up through the constituency parties. (It was, of course, this feature of the Labour Party in the thirties, not any revolutionary activity amongst the ranks of organised labour, which made the thirties for so long the 'Golden Decade' to so many on the left.) But, however this may be, my point here is that the analytic distinction I have drawn between doctrine and ethos did not, at that time, correspond to different parts of the party. Each part of the ideology affected the thinking of each part of the party.

Much the same was true of the period of wartime coalition. It was not the case, as many thought until recently, that the tools of ideological conflict were put away for the period of the war. It could, indeed, be argued that the Conservative Party put its ideological tools away while Labour kept its workshop in working order. A recent historian of the period, Paul Addison, has argued that Labour's great electoral victory of 1945, and its subsequent ability to legislate the welfare state and make that legislation stick, was largely due to the ideological somnolence of the Conservative Party in the war years.[1] Labour kept on producing plans, kept up-to-date with the plans and ideas others were producing (most importantly with the Beveridge Report) and kept in touch with the mood of its supporters and the country. The Opposition did not. In this period Labour had it all ways. Its opponents both in the Conservative Party and the Communist Party ceased hostilities, but Labour kept moving; it enjoyed the advantages of government (and, most sweetly, the advantages of government without serious parliamentary opposition or, thanks to American financial support, the need to worry about money) without suffering the opprobrium of making unpopular government decisions. It became so closely associated with the government and the war effort that it was no longer easy to use the symbols of nationhood against it; and yet it was blamed by no one for the failures of government. Most of all, the period of coalition government served to disguise the dilemmas of simultaneously representing a class interest and being responsible for the governing of the whole country. For this reason the war was a kind of ideological holiday for the Labour Party.

That holiday came to an abrupt end with the electoral victory of 1945. The euphoria of the victory, the achievements of the first few years – the creation of the national health service, the nationalisation of the mines, independence for India – served at first to keep the underlying tensions hidden. But it was in this period that the conflicts between the responsibility to govern and the responsibility to create socialism became sharper. In the two previous periods of government the conflicts could always be explained away by the fact that the government was in a minority (and in 1924 it was not even the largest party). But after 1945 that excuse was no longer available: the government had to begin to explain why it was making non-socialist choices. The choice of the United States rather than the Soviet Union as a primary ally could be defended on many grounds; but not on socialist grounds. Decisions which followed from this decision, about the rearmament of Germany, the entry into the Korean War, the creation of NATO, were not easily accepted by the movement. Other decisions taken towards the end of the Attlee governments, especially the decision to make 'our' health service impose charges, gave rise to real doubts, while the failure to nationalise sugar and the delay in nationalising steel were omens whose portent was not lost. Still, the 1945–51 governments were immensely popular with Labour's voters. Labour has never again won so high a number of votes or so large a proportion of the poll as it did in 1951 (when it lost).

In the thirteen years which followed, the fundamental weaknesses of Labour's two doctrinal strands – egalitarianism and planning socialism – were exposed to view. This period in opposition, particularly after the defeats of 1955 and 1959, bore some resemblance to the period after 1931. The parliamentary leadership had trouble (less than in the thirties, but still real trouble) in asserting control over the movement in the country. The great debates over unilateral disarmament, which Gaitskell and his allies eventually won, and over Clause 4, which they lost, showed that the party could stand up to its leaders. In both cases the battle was won by the section of the party which urged the party's traditional values. It was lost by the doctrinaires. I have no wish to celebrate either victory (I would have been on the losing side both times), but that is not the point. My point here is that the movement did not sort itself, in the 'Thirteen Wasted Years', into a 'doctrine' section and an 'ethos' section. Moreover, its ethos remained coherent – Labour governments had not been sufficiently common or long-lasting to lure a significant section of the party away from the old defensive working-class ethos.

But the tensions first exposed in the years of Opposition have become painfully obvious in the years (mainly in government) which have followed. Labour has remained the party of equality, in large part, as I have argued, because it has suited both its own doctrinaires and the propagandists of the Conservative Party. But it has, in government, all but forsaken its right to be proud of its record on this subject. The government policy which has done most for equality is full employment. Britain is not an equal society if equality means equality of income; neither is it appreciably more equal in this respect than it was before Labour came to power. Britain is not importantly more equal in opportunities for poorer citizens to join the middle class; and what progress there has been in this respect is not unambiguously to be credited to the Labour Party – or to the movement. But full employment is a policy which the movement demanded and a Labour government created and then enshrined in a principle so popular that Conservative governments did not dare tamper with it. Full employment perhaps made little difference to equality of income; but it made a considerable difference to equality of regard. And Labour's achievement here was real. But in government since 1967, and increasingly since 1974, the Labour Party has come to accept a high rate of unemployment as normal. At the end of 1977 approximately 6 per cent of the work-force were registered for unemployment benefit; this is about 1½ million people, and there are certainly many more also without work who do not register. Few protests about this are heard; and this relative silence is the greatest change which has overtaken the Labour Party and, more important, the Labour movement in recent years. It is not simply a matter of not wanting to embarrass 'our' government, though there is an element of that. Rather, it is that the movement has lost its will to fight unemployment. It lacks any conviction on this subject. The movement is much more concerned, and is seen to be more concerned, with preserving existing jobs and raising the wages of those already in work than with the plight of the unemployed. Emblematically, it has great difficulty in encouraging the sharing of work, because the pressure from those in work who want their overtime money is greater than the pressure from those out of work who need any job.

This is a change of conviction which has not gone unnoticed by the unemployed – especially by the many young people who are unemployed. A recent report of a job creation scheme in Sunderland quotes one young man who said: 'They all talk about the Jarrow march, but they think we ask to doss about.' Another said of the trade unions: 'They are a club for the employed. They call you brother and sister. I wouldn't leave mine out in the cold.'[2] He might well have added that a party and a movement which do leave their brothers and sisters out in the cold at once abandon their right to speak for equality and risk losing an important part of their support.

Martin Walker's recent studies of the National Front show that the Front is gaining support from precisely this group in society. Walker has observed:

It is significant that this growing NF [National Front] appeal in the inner cities has come at a time of economic recession, with unemployment rising to 1,500,000 and successive cuts in public expenditure reducing the money available to improve the housing, the health care, education and social services available to deprived areas.

He goes on to remark tellingly:

. . . the NF [is] an organised political party moving into a political vacuum. Labour's traditional control of the East End [of London] had been so secure for so long that the political machine atrophied, particularly when de-industrialisation removed much of the trade union base. . . . In strong Labour areas, like the mining regions of Durham or the London docks, the Labour Party and the trade union had traditionally been more than the dominant political force in the community: they had also been key vehicles of education, of recreation, of social life. By the 1970s the Labour organisations in the inner cities had begun to look like rotten boroughs.[3]

A party and a movement which forsake their original crusade for a self-satisfied role as the natural party of government risk just such rottenness at their base. Labour has had a change of heart here. A Labour government has acted on the Conservative belief that unemployment will fall only after the rate of inflation has been controlled. This change of heart has deprived the party of the right to claim to

110 *Doctrine and Ethos in the Labour Party*

be the party of equality; and even the mutual interest of the Conservative and Labour leaders in keeping Labour labelled as the party of equality will not long serve to hide the change.

The experience of government in the years after 1964 has also done much to deprive Labour of the right to equate its socialism with planning. As we noticed in Chapter 4, the Labour government of 1954–51 has already abandoned the stricter planning controls which it had inherited from the wartime administration in favour of the looser controls of Keynesian economic planning and land-use control. But the difficulties of co-ordinating all of the multifarious activities and responsibilities of government are now overwhelming. The excesses of capitalism, such as competition and waste, which the Labour ideologists of the 1920s and 1930s sought to eliminate by the application of state control have largely been transferred into the government machinery itself. The large agencies of government are too large to be treated solely as instruments of government policy. They have wills of their own. As a result, the notion that the overall effect of government activity can be to plan social change is incredible. Since 1974 Labour governments have hardly even bothered to pretend that they believe it themselves.

They have also (though this is quite a different argument) been forced by membership of the EEC to give up some other tools of economic planning. The policy of paying regional employment premiums to firms who operate in the economically depressed regions of Britain was ended for this reason. The party has also given in to the demand for strong devolved assemblies in Scotland and Wales. This concession will make the central planning of the economy and the provision of uniform social services all over the country (always a bit of a myth, but a noble myth for all that) impossible to sustain.

It would perhaps be possible to claim these concessions as deliberate changes in the character of Labour's socialism, or as conscious shifts of emphasis within its doctrines, were it not for the fact that they are all rather too obviously concessions to contingent political pressures; and were it not for the fact that the concessions Labour has made are adequately explained on the basis of quite conventional political self-interest without need to recur to any facet of the party's ideology. The effect had been to water down the party's commitment to the two main strands in its doctrine. It has thereby become all but doctrineless.

The most painful adjustment of the party in this period of power has been made, I have argued, by the party's ministers. It is they who have to face both their unreconstructed constituency parties and the reality of power in a bourgeois world without the aid of a specifically socialist ethos and with a threadbare series of doctrines. They have become co-opted into the system and cease for anything other than ritualistic purposes to pay obeisance to the old ethos. They like the power game; their liking is reinforced by the fact that they are coming to play it rather well. This is all very well, but it opens up, for the first time in the history of the party, a gap between those who operate within the terms of the party's ethos, the constituency parties, and those who march to new tunes. For the party's parliamentary group it often seems that neither the party's doctrines nor its defensive ethos have any impact. For its constituency parties it seems that both continue to operate, if in a muted way.

It is surely no accident that the most controversial constitutional change now on the agenda of the party has been raised by a group of constituency parties. It concerns their rights in the selection and reselection of Labour Party parliamentary candidates. This process is the crux of the relationship between the parliamentary party and the party in the country. It is also the source of considerable ill will and misunderstanding.

At present, roughly two-thirds of United Kingdom parliamentary seats are safely in the hands of one party or other. Of these, about half (i.e. one-third of the total – say, 210) are safe Labour seats. In theory all Labour seats are equal in regard to candidate selection: the general management committee of each constituency chooses its candidate before each general election. In fact, there is an important difference between those seats which regularly return Labour MPs and those which do not.

Where there is no Labour MP the system actually works rather as it is supposed to: the GMC selects a new candidate for each general election. The previous candidate may be reselected but he has no privileged access to the nomination. He must go through the same procedures as everyone else. In any case, previous candidates do not normally wish to recontest seats they have already lost, preferring instead to look for more winnable prospects. Thus, in safe non-Labour seats, the GMC exercises its right to select its certain loser before each general election unimpeded.

Where there is a Labour MP, however, the practice is quite different. Unless the constituency party takes positive action to prevent it he is, in effect, automatically reselected. Unless, that is, the GMC passes a motion of no confidence in him, no selection procedure is put into effect until the Prime Minister announces the date for the next election. By then it is impossible to do anything other than reselect the sitting MP: a full selection process takes several months and is so unsettling that no constituency party would go through it on the eve of a general election if it could help it. There are no formal rules barring a GMC from deciding not to reselect; but reselection has to be approved by the National Executive Committee. The NEC vets all newly chosen candidates. This used to be a way of ensuring that communists and other trouble-makers were not selected. It is now mainly a way of ensuring that GMCs follow the procedural rules correctly in selecting their candidates. To help ensure this, the NEC insists on having a paid central official, such as the regional organiser or a member of the regional Labour Party executive present when the selection is made. Usually, his presence is sufficient to dissuade a GMC from trying to unseat its MP if the MP wishes to be reselected. Through such informal processes constituency parties in safe Labour seats only actually get to choose a candidate when the sitting MP relinquishes his seat. It is against this immobility, and against MPs' increasingly resented social and intellectual distance from the GMCs who originally selected them, that GMCs now chafe.

This is a sign of an interesting change in the ideology of the movement. The demand to end automatic reselection goes directly counter to the previously dominant feeling that once a man had a job he should not be booted out. In the new demand we see the emergence, at GMC level, of a new ethos. Or, rather, we hear the final echoes of the old defensive working-class ethos being overwhelmed by the stronger beat of new tunes. It is perhaps no accident that these signs are apparent at a time when the individual membership of the Labour Party is declining and the only source of new recruitment into the party comes from the young, often well-educated, frequently very left-wing activists. These new recruits, often the children of working-class homes, no longer march to the old tunes, any more than the MPs do. The strongest tune in the new ethos these younger members march to is 'democracy'. They would like to make MPs and councillors more directly accountable to their local parties; make the Labour Party's parliamentary and local government groups more collectively accountable to the party's manifesto; have some say in the choice of the parliamentary leader and generally reduce the scope that MPs and councillors enjoy to interpret the will of the party. They are completely lacking in the feeling which their elders had that party officials and MPs have a right to stay in their jobs if they want to carry on. The MPs are treated more as office-holders than as comrades. At the same time, then, that MPs and Labour cabinets are uncomfortably shifting away from the old defensive ethos, and more and more openly coming to admit and face up to their liking for power and for the accoutrements of power, the GMCs are also moving away from the same ethos. But, in doing this, the GMCs are coming into conflict with MPs in a way previously not known in the Labour Party. Both parts of the party are abandoning the old ethos; both are acquiring more of the feelings and habits of a self-confident ruling party; and both are determined to deny that they have changed. Both insist that their present position is consistent with the basic ideals and beliefs of the party's founders.

It is not difficult, if we reflect on the likely consequences of the increasingly open ideological divisions within the Labour Party, to see that a number of conflicts will result. The conflict between GMCs and MPs (many of whom favour automatic reselection) has already been mentioned. There is also a demand that the party choose its leader in a more democratic way. At present both the Conservative and Liberal parties have more democratic methods of choosing their leaders which involve party members other than MPs. This comparison rankles with many of Labour's supporters who are not accustomed to belonging to the least democratic major party. On the other hand, the Parliamentary Labour Party can be depended upon to fight to retain its sole right to choose the leader of the party. But its position will be undermined by external constitutional changes. There will soon be a Labour group leader in the European Parliament. It is not difficult to foresee the demand that the NEC or even annual conference have a role in choosing him. Whoever chooses him, he will not take lightly to the notion that the leader of the PLP is his leader. Why should he? Similarly, the Scottish and Welsh assemblies (if created) will have Labour groups with leaders. The assembly groups will lack the prestige of the PLP and may find it difficult to monopolise the choice of leader. If they have to share the decision with other bodies, the analogy will soon be applied to Parliament; and, in any case, the relative power of the leader of the PLP (even if he is Prime Minister) will decline as all these new bodies acquire authority.

More fundamental is the increasing weakness of the Labour Party in elections. Its support has dropped considerably, if unevenly, from the peak at the 1951 general election. The proportion of the vote won by Labour since the 1950 general election is:

1950	1951	1955	1959	1964	1966	1970
46·1	48·8	46·4	43·9	44·1	48·1	43·1
		1974(Feb.)		1974(Oct.)		
		37·2		39·2		

The party's vote as a percentage of the electorate has also declined and tells an even sadder tale:

38·7	40·3	35·6	34·5	34·0	36·4	31·0
		29·3		28·6		

The party has been able to form governments on the basis of these decreasing votes because opposition to it is divided and because the Conservative Party has also lost voters in large numbers. The number of MPs elected by the party has not dropped in step with the loss of voters:

LABOUR MPs

1950	1951	1955	1959	1964	1966	1970
315	295	277	258	317	364	288

1974(Feb.)	1974(Oct.)
301	319

Thus the electoral system and the failure of Labour's opponents have acted to disguise the problem. How long the party can continue to elect large numbers of MPs on a decreasing vote is open to question.

Indeed, there is now considerable survey evidence which suggests that the move of voters away from the Labour Party is not a transitory phenomenon. It is a reflection of the weakening of the social system which supported strong loyalty to the party in the past. In 1974, Professor Rose devised a measure of intra-party cohesion on various issues. He found that Conservative voters were more likely to agree with each other than Labour voters (41 to 25 per cent). The disagreement between Labour voters on key issues was shown by the fact that on eight issues – steel nationalisation, the power of the unions, internment in Ulster, housing, taxation, Britain's world role, abortion and commercial radio – there was no majority opinion amongst Labour voters. Rose also discovered that Labour voters tended to agree slightly more with Conservative MPs than Labour MPs on the major policy issues.[4] These findings point up the disagreements between Labour voters and the party they support. And they highlight how important other factors are in leading people to vote Labour.

The most important other factor is, of course, the feeling among large numbers of voters that Labour is their party; that Labour represents their interests. It is here that the results of the research carried out by Ivor Crewe and his team are so poignant. Crewe found that for many voters the February 1974 election was the 'last straw'. They abandoned their traditional party because they were hostile to the disruptive powers of the trade unions and to the unions' close involvement in the Labour Party. Crewe *et al.* also found that Labour (and, for that matter, Conservative) voters were decreasingly inclined to associate their class and their party. As they say:

. . . the fall in support for Labour party principles amongst its own identifiers – in particular its younger, working-class and trade-unionist 'core' – [has] particular significance. For it is difficult to conceive of a party avoiding a long-term electoral decline if the majority of its surviving supporters reject the majority of its basic policies. The position of the Labour Party is likely to be particularly precarious after a spell in government in which it disappoints the economic expectations of its voters. For when a party's followers no longer feel the same strength of attachment, largely reject its policies, and believe their economic interests have been failed, what is left to attract their vote?[5]

This can be put another way: the increasingly self-confident socialism of the Labour Party's activists is in conflict, on the one hand, with the ideas of the parliamentary party and, on the other hand, with the ideas of the electorate. Even the more tepidly socialist ideas of the PLP are too much for the electorate. We may wonder if a party whose activists are so far removed from the ideas of the voters can long continue to hope to gain access to the levers of power through the ballot-box.

This query is related to another. Labour's ideology is firmly based on the supremacy in Britain of the decisions made in Parliament. The whole notion, as I have argued, that it is worth trying to achieve socialism through the democratic process is predicated on the idea that the winner in the democratic process can make fundamental changes in British society. Left-wing socialists have never really been convinced that this parliamentary aspect of Labour's ideology makes much sense. They have always believed that British capitalism is quite capable of erecting extra-parliamentary – if need be, extra-legal – barriers to thwart the will of a socialist Parliament. These doubts about the efficacy of Parliament have been substantially boosted by recent events. There is, first of all, the not inconsiderable shift of sovereignty to the institutions of the Common Market and away from Parliament to reckon with. Secondly, Parliament may be about to devolve some of its authority to two assemblies – one for Scotland and one for Wales. However temporary such devolution may be in law, it will prove impossible in fact to recall the power devolved. Parliamentary sovereignty has also been undermined by the introduction – by the Labour Party, it should be said – of referenda. As yet no Parliament has legally bound itself to obey the result of a referendum; but ignoring such a result would be a dangerous course for any government to follow.

All of these developments have reduced the importance of decisions taken in Parliament by the elected representatives of the people. And it has been a notable feature of the parliamentary debates on these subjects that some of the strongest opposition to these various constitutional changes has come from the old left of the Labour Party, from the remnants of the Bevanites – for they have been admirably consistent in their belief in the sovereignty of Parliament. None the less these are all changes which have been brought about by Parliament itself; and, indeed, others are already on the agenda and may be enacted. Devolution to English regional assemblies is one possibility.

But parliamentary sovereignty, and with it the parliamentarianism of the Labour Party, is being threatened by more fundamental changes than these, changes which have been forced on Parliament by outside agencies – some of them part of the Labour movement. The locus of decision-making in Britain is moving far beyond the bounds of Westminster. Negotiations about many of the important issues of the day do not take place within the Houses of Parliament. Even if we leave aside the impact on British public policy of foreign governments and international private corporations and international government agencies – though their collective impact is considerable – there are many domestic pressure-groups which must be placated outside parliament. Some now argue that Britain is a 'corporate state' – that is, that the main bargains are struck between government on the one hand and large corporations and unions on the other.[6] That important bargains, about such crucial issues as pay policy, are struck in this way cannot be doubted. When this happens the government of the day simply presents the result to Parliament. It does not consult Parliament or change its own bargaining position as the result of parliamentary pressure. Mr Heath's campaign for re-election in February 1974 on the issue 'Who runs Britain?' highlighted this fact without changing it. Whichever party formed a government after the February 1974 election knew that one of its first tasks would be to settle with the miners.

The February 1974 election, and especially Heath's emphasis on his fight with the miners over their pay claim, shocked many political commentators. As a result a number of people started asking, 'Is Britain ungovernable?'[7] The fear that it might be arose from the realisation that Britain was no longer being governed by Parliament, and that a Conservative government, in particular, could no longer rule simply by virtue of having a majority of seats in the House of Commons. As we have seen, some left-wing critics of the Labour Party have argued that Labour governments have *always* faced this problem. Now the shoe was on the other foot – and it pinched. The willingness of the miners – but not the miners alone, also the engineers and the power workers – to use their industrial muscle on behalf of the Labour Party in the early 1970s emphasised the impotence of Parliament.

The willingness of these major unions to do business on a reasonably amicable basis with the Labour government which followed the February 1974 election answered the question 'Is Britain ungovernable?' Britain is governable by a Labour government (even one that has a negligible or non-existent majority in the House of Commons) backed by the trade union movement. In the first instance this answer will be most gratifying to the Labour Party – and it is a new factor which the party will certainly use to advantage in future elections. But that immediate partisan advantage is insignificant beside the important change in the British constitution which it signals. Britain is moving from parliamentary democracy to corporate democracy. In these new circumstances it may be more important to know which powerful interest-groups are united with which political parties than to know which party has won most votes or holds the most seats in the House of Commons. Labour is the immediate beneficiary of this change. My strong impression is that it will adjust its ideology to this new world more easily than will the Conservative Party. After all, Labour began as the parliamentary expression of the trade union movement. Now what it must do is readjust to this former role. But if it is to adjust it must abandon its parliamentarianism – its Bevanite belief that important decisions are made, or will be defended, on the floor of the House of Commons.

This important shift can be analysed in different terms: Labour's ideology is based on the two-party electoral system. The basis of manifestoism is that the Labour Party will from time to time form a government of its own unaided by any other party after a general election victory. It presumes that the party leaders will not have to trade policies with the leaders of other parties in order to form coalition governments; and it presumes that these leaders will not have to, in effect, form coalitions with extra parliamentary pressure-groups to carry out the party's will as government. Both these assumptions are now exposed as inadequate, for the two-party system is faltering. In the general election of 1951, when the two-party system was at its strongest, 82·6 per cent of those on the electoral register voted and 96 per cent of them voted for one of the two major parties. Both these figures have been dropping since. In the most recent general election 72·8 per cent of the people voted – 75 per cent of them for one of the two major parties. In the Parliament formed after the 1951 election only nine MPs were from 'minor' parties; in the Parliament formed after the October 1974 election there were thirty-nine MPs from the no longer so minor parties. Thus, formal coalitions may soon be necessary to create a parliamentary majority.

The major victim of these changes has so far been the Conservative Party. For that party was not simply one of the two major parties in a two-party system; it was the natural party of government. It had successfully attached to itself all of the symbols of patriotism – or at least of English patriotism. Its platforms were often draped with the Union Jack. Its dominance was such that as recently as the 1959–64 Parliament prominent Labour ideologists such as R. H. S. Crossman accepted the Conservatives' right to rule and thought that Labour would – and should – only come to office when the Conservatives had made an uncharacteristic mess.[8] This predominance of the Conservative Party was manifest in their unwillingness to lower themselves to appeal to the electorates in ideological terms. They put themselves forward as the party of the whole nation.[9] They were much less willing than Labour to make promises in opposition (which they rarely had to endure) which they would have trouble fulfilling in office. This is no longer the case. Both Mr Heath and Mrs Thatcher have made specific promises to specific groups while they have been leaders of the

Opposition. The Conservative Party's painful shift from being the natural party of government to being just another pressure-group party has gathered pace as Labour has remained in office. In 1978, Mrs Thatcher – frightened by her party's poor showing in the opinion polls? – was moved to play the race-card. She abandoned the tacit bi-partisan agreement not to stir up racial fears and implied that her party would stop immigration and even begin repatriation of black Britons if returned to office. Such promises will make it more difficult both for her and the party convincingly to portray themselves as the natural rulers of all the people. The willingness of Conservative Party leaders to make such promises is a sign of the party's abandonment of its previous role and its adoption of the role of one party fighting for support amongst many.

But the rapid change brought about by the ending of the two-party system, and the consequent need for the old parties to adjust, has not left Labour unscathed. One result of the changed situation is a weakening of party discipline amongst MPs. Like the Conservative government of 1970-4, the Labour government which followed it lost several measures on which it had imposed a three-line whip on its MPs. The Heath government lost such a vote on its draft Immigration Rules in 1972. Against the traditional expectation the government did not resign. When MPs of both parties saw this they felt freer to vote against their whips. In 1973, the Heath government failed to get its way in the House of Commons on two occasions. Only three months after Labour was returned with a majority in October 1974 its MPs showed that they had learned the lessons: the government was defeated in January 1975 on the Report stage of the Social Security Benefits Bill. In July 1975, it was defeated on an Opposition amendment to the Finance Bill (the first time a government had been defeated on a Finance Bill without immediately resigning) and in August on a clause in the Housing Finance (Special Provisions) Bill. After this government defeats became all but commonplace. In the session 1976-7 the government had to withdraw its Scotland and Wales Bill after it failed to get a guillotine – because of abstentions or votes against it by forty-three Labour MPs. In 1977-8, its replacement for Scotland, the Scotland Bill, was amended six times against the government's will – and few ill effects were felt by those MPs who voted against their whips.

Party discipline is weakening amongst MPs at the same time that it is weakening amongst the voters. One reason for the weakening of discipline amongst MPs may well be the electorate's new liberality. No longer need a renegade MP abandon all hope of being returned to Parliament. In the 1970 general election, S. O. Davies won an overwhelming victory in his old seat of Merthyr Tydfil after the Labour Party had refused to reselect him. Davies's was the first such election victory by a renegade since 1945. In 1973, Dick Taverne went one better. He had resigned as the Labour MP for Lincoln in October 1972 as the result of a long-standing dispute with his constituency association. At the March 1973 by-election caused by his resignation he formed a new party – the Lincoln Democratic Labour Association – and won the seat with an increased vote. This was the first time an independent candidate had won a by-election since the war. Since that time two other breakaway political parties have been formed around dissident Labour MPs. Eddie Milne won Blyth as an Independent Labour candidate in the February 1974 election, and Jim Sillars and John Robertson (South Ayrshire and Paisley respectively) formed a breakaway Scottish Labour Party in 1976, though they declined to resign their seats which they had won as Labour candidates.[10] These breakaway parties have had mixed success at local government elections. Taverne's party has been the most successful. It captured control of Lincoln District Council and increased its majority in 1976. Milne's party has captured seats in Blyth. The Scottish Labour Party, on the other hand, won only three district seats in all of Scotland in the elections held in May 1977. These achievements, while hardly earth-shattering, do suggest that in propitious circumstances such parties can find a place in the party system. They thus pose a threat to the Labour Movement's solidarity.

So strong are the old assumptions that the import of the weakening of the two-party system has only just begun to sink home. The belief that Britain is inevitably a two-party country is deep-seated, and there is a strong inclination to treat any deviation as either minor or temporary. This inclination still predominates in the Labour Party. These attitudes would be shattered, however, if future Labour leaders were forced to negotiate a formal coalition with the leaders of other parties. We have seen the damage to Labour's ideology caused by the need to compromise in power as a result of the constraints imposed on Labour ministers by their civil servants. Further damage could be done by the sight of Labour's leaders negotiating with leaders of other parties for cabinet posts, and over which parts of Labour's manifesto to jettison publically. The memory of the 1931 'betrayal' could easily be invoked.

Yet it was noticeable that the 'pact' agreed by Mr Callaghan and Mr Steel in 1977, according to which Labour won Liberal support for its continuation in power in return for an agreement to consult with the Liberal leaders on the whole range of government policy, raised suspicion but impressively little fuss in the party. It is true that this pact did not require formal abandonment of any cherished politics, but its acceptance by the party may betoken a further weakening of the old working-class ethos – for nothing better exemplified that ethos than the determination built up after the 1931 débâcle never to form a government again without a parliamentary majority.

We may speculate that this weakening may tempt another generation of social democrats to try to wrench the party away from its past – to try to refight and win the battle of 1959 over Clause 4. But surely this would be a mistake. In the present circumstances any attempt by the doctrinaire social democratic right to assert their own position would be welcomed by the doctrinaire fundamentalist left as an opportunity for them to unite with the trade unions in the centre and isolate those on the right. At the same time, any attempt by the doctrinaire left to move the party in its direction would threaten the party with electoral disaster. As we have seen, the party is already to the left of its electorate. Indeed, at the risk of being unkind, it could be suggested that both groups of doctrinaires would be better employed rethinking their doctrines than trying to win the party to what are, by now, rather threadbare ideas.

But this double bind need not be too worrying for, whatever may happen in the next few years, the basis of two-party electoral politics has been eroded. The collective popularity of the Liberals, Scottish and Welsh Nationalists, the Irish parties and the National Front is considerable and will not disappear. And with the erosion of two-party competition has gone the need for the Labour Party (or the Conservative Party, for that matter) to try to build a majority coalition of electors. Indeed, given that the need to build such a coalition of voters is past, it is even a bit foolhardy to try, because in trying to please too many voters the party could end by alienating its strongest supporters. We may, I think, further speculate that in the emerging multi-party world each party will need a strong core of support most of all – not a majority or near-majority of votes. And at the same time it will have less need for its doctrinaires and policy-writers, for in a multi-party world the manifestos of the parties will be but bargaining-counters which will be traded for Cabinet seats by the party leaders after each election. Thus, at the same time as Labour's doctrines are revealed to be threadbare, those who write them are losing their usefulness to the party. Labour, with its solid support in the trade union movement and its ideology securely founded on the ethos of trade unionists, ought to be able to play the new multi-party game to advantage.

If the party can retain these traditional supports, it could, indeed, emerge not simply as one large party in a multi-party state but as the natural coalition partner in whatever coalition is being formed after each election. For every government will have to do business with the trade unions, and Labour has a special relationship here. Even the occasional majority Conservative governments will have learned this lesson from the 1970s. But perhaps the greatest losers from these changes will be Labour's own doctrinaires, for their role will have been reduced almost to insignificance.

NOTES

1   Addison, P., *The Road to 1945* (London, 1975).
2   'Springboard: a study of CSV's job creation project in Sunderland', quoted in the *Guardian*, 10 February 1978, p. 4.
3   Walker, M., 'The National Front', in Drucker, H. M. (ed.), *Multi-Party Britain* (forthcoming).
4   Rose, R., *The Problem of Party Government* (Harmondsworth, 1974), p. 301.
5   Crewe, I., *et al.*, 'Partisan Dealignment in Britain 1964–71', *British Journal of Political Science*, vol. 7, 1977, p. 187.
6   See Ionescue, G., *Centripetal Politics: Government and the New Centres of Power* (London, 1975).
7   For a discussion of this question, see King, A. (ed.), *Why Is Britain Becoming Harder to Govern?* (London, 1976).
8   Howell, D., *British Social Democracy* (London, 1976), p. 229.
9   See Gamble, A., 'The Conservative Party', in Drucker, *Multi-Party Britain*.
10 See Drucker, H. M., *Breakaway: The Scottish Labour Party* (Edinburgh, 1978), and Milne, E., *No Shining Armour* (London, 1976).

Appendix
Chronology of Events Significant
to the History of the Labour Party

1900   Labour Representation Committee is founded in London by representatives of the TUC, the Independent Labour Party (ILP), and the Social Democratic Foundation (SDF). Ramsay MacDonald is elected secretary. LRC fields fifteen candidates in October general election; two, Keir Hardie and Richard Bell, win.

1906   Labour puts up fifty candidates in general election; twenty-nine win – mostly with the assistance of the Liberal Party. The MPs rename their group 'The Labour Party'. Keir Hardie is chosen chairman.

1910   In January, Labour wins forty seats in seventy-eight contests. George Barnes is elected chairman. In December, the party wins forty-two of fifty-six contests.

1911   MacDonald elected chairman.

1912   Trade union affiliation begins to rise sharply and continues to rise until postwar trade depression of 1920.

1914   Many in the party, including MacDonald, are opposed to the war. Arthur Henderson, who is not opposed to the war, assumes chairmanship from MacDonald.

1915   Henderson joins the government and the Cabinet. Government hopes thereby to still Labour unrest. The hope is not fulfilled.

1916   Lloyd George forms a government which includes three Labour ministers.

1917   Russian Revolution begins. W. Adamson succeeds Henderson as chairman.

1918   War ends. Party adopts new constitution which gives trade unions entrenched position and explicitly (Clause 4) commits the party to socialism. Labour wins fifty-seven seats in 361 contests.

1920   Communist Party is formed. Its application for affiliation to the Labour Party is rejected.

1921   Postwar trade recession. Membership of TUC and trade union membership of the Labour Party begin to drop. Talk of General Strike is common. J. R. Clynes becomes chairman.

1922   Labour almost trebles parliamentary representation to 142 seats in 441 contests. New PLP narrowly elects MacDonald as its 'chairman and leader'. Labour nearly doubles vote from 1918 and replaces Liberals as second party for the first time. (Henceforth alternation in two-party system is between Labour and Conservative.)

1923   Conservative Prime Minister Baldwin calls December election. Labour gains seats; wins 191 out of 427 contests. Conservatives still largest party.

1924   Labour forms first minority administration. Philip Snowden becomes Chancellor; Henderson is Home Secretary; MacDonald is Prime Minister and Foreign Secretary. New election is forced in October. Labour wins 151 seats from 514 contests. Conservatives form government.

1926 General Strike in May. Miners carry on strike after other workers return. Miners eventually forced back on owners' terms. Party plays small role.

1929 Labour benefits from unpopularity of Conservative government, particularly because of its failure to do anything about unemployment. Labour wins 287 seats from 569 contests and becomes, for the first time, the largest party in the House of Commons. Second MacDonald minority administration formed. Henderson becomes Foreign Secretary. Snowden is again Chancellor; J. H. Thomas becomes Lord Privy Seal. Sidney Webb and Oswald Mosley are also ministers.

1931 MacDonald resigns office in August. His Cabinet resigns, too. MacDonald then forms Conservative-dominated 'National' government; Snowden and Thomas join as well. Labour reduced in October election to forty-six seats (plus six seats held by unendorsed Labour candidates) in 491 contests. Henderson becomes leader.

1932 Henderson resigns as leader; George Lansbury elected.

1935 Clem Attlee elected leader after Lansbury humiliated by Ernest Bevin. At general election Labour recovers most of its 1929 vote, but wins only 154 seats from 539 contests.

1936 Labour does nothing about the Spanish Civil War although some individual members go to fight.

1939 War with Germany breaks out. Communists hinder war effort.

1940 Labour brings down Chamberlain government with renegade Conservative help. Labour joins National Government, under Churchill. Attlee, Arthur Greenwood, Bevin and Herbert Morrison all given prominent government jobs.

1941 The Soviet Union – after attack by Germany – and the United States – after attack by Japan – join war effort.

1945 Germany surrenders in May. General election in July. Labour wins first overall majority. Takes 393 seats from 604 contests. Attlee becomes Prime Minister; Bevin is Foreign Secretary; Morrison is Lord President; Greenwood is Lord Privy Seal (with responsibility for the social services); Dalton becomes Chancellor. Aneurin Bevan enters government as Minister of Housing.

1946-7 Government nationalises the railways, coal, the Bank of England and some road transport. In November 1946, NHS is created.

1947-8 Gas and electricity nationalised. Severe winter of 1947-8 compounds currency crisis and increased dependence on USA government begins to falter.

1950 Labour retains majority at general election with 315 seats (to the Conservatives' 298) in 617 contests.

1951 Labour wins highest ever vote (13,948,385), but Conservatives win more seats and inaugurate thirteen successive years of government. Labour wins 295 seats in 617 contests.

1955 Conservatives increase their majority at general election. Labour wins 277 seats in 620 contests. Hugh Gaitskell succeeds Attlee as leader. Morrison and Bevan are defeated candidates. Within the party a split develops between a Gaitskellite (or revisionist) right and a Bevanite (or fundamentalist) left.

1956   Britain 'invades' Egypt at Suez in collusion with France and Israel. Labour unites behind its leaders in revulsion at Tory imperialism.

1959   Conservatives increase seats again at general election. Labour despondent. Gaitskell blames defeat on Clause 4; at special conference asks for it to be modified. He fails.

1960   Gaitskell's enemies and others persuade annual conference to support policy of unilateral nuclear disarmament for Britain. Bevan dies.

1961   Annual conference reverses decision about unilateral nuclear disarmament.

1963   Wilson succeeds to leadership on Gaitskell's death. George Brown (the original favourite) and James Callaghan are defeated candidates.

1964   Labour returns to office with overall majority of six seats. Labour wins 317 of 628 contests. Wilson becomes Prime Minister; Callaghan is Chancellor; Brown becomes Minister for Economic Affairs. Patrick Gordon Walker becomes Foreign Secretary; Denis Healey is Defence Secretary.

1966   Labour wins large majority at general election – taking 363 seats from 621 contests. Government spends much time and money trying to protect the value of the pound.

1967   Pound is devalued. Unpopular government begins to lose by-elections.

1969   Government proposals to reform law on trade unions embodied in the White Paper *In Place of Strife* are strongly opposed by unions and eventually dropped.

1970   Despite favourable opinion-polls, Labour loses office. Wins 287 seats from 624 contests. Conservative government proposes trade union legislation similar to that outlined by Labour.

1971   Conservative proposals enacted as Industrial Relations Act.

1972   Britain joins the Common Market. Miners' strike humiliates government into conceding pay demand.

1973   Miners strike again.

1974   In February, with the miners still on strike and the country working three days a week to conserve fuel, the government calls a general election on 'Who runs Britain?' issue. Minority Labour administration returned. Labour wins 301 seats from 623 contests. In October, Labour wins 319 seats from 623 contests and forms majority administration. Repeals Industrial Relations Act. Forms 'Social Contract' with General Council of TUC.

1975   Britain votes in referendum to remain in EEC.

1976   Wilson resigns as leader; Callaghan succeeds him. Michael Foot is runner-up. Government loses overall majority in House of Commons.

1977   Government forms 'pact' with Liberals. Liberal support for certain legislation agreed. Ulster Unionists provide tacit support. They hope that Ulster representation at Westminster will be increased. Scottish National Party and Plaid Cymru also provide tacit support in return for promise of devolution.

SOURCES: H. Pelling, *A Short History of the Labour Party* and F. W. S. Craig, *British Political Facts 1885–1975*.

Bibliography

This select bibliography contains only the works I have found useful generally in the preparation of this book. I have not cited the works used only once or twice.

General Theory

Bell, D., *The End of Ideology or the Exhaustion of Political Ideas in the Fifties* (London, 1962).

Berki, R. N., *Socialism* (London, 1975).

Hobsbawm, E. J., 'The social functions of the past: some questions', *Past and Present*, no. 55, pp. 3–17.

Kolakowski, L., and Hampshire, S., *The Socialist Idea: A Reappraisal* (London, 1974).

Lichtheim, G., *A Short History of Socialism* (London, 1970).

Michels, R., *Political Parties: A Sociological Study of the Oligarchical Tendencies of Modern Democracy* (New York, 1959).

Miliband, R., 'Analysing the bourgeois state', *New Left Review*, no. 82, November–December 1973, pp. 83–93.

Miliband, R., and Poulantzas, N., 'The problem of the capitalist state (an exchange)', in Blackburn, R. (ed.), *Ideology in Social Science* (London, 1972), pp. 238–64.

Nettle, P., 'The German Social Democratic Party 1890–1914 as a policital model', *Past and Present*, no. 30, April 1965, pp. 65–94.

Ostrogorski, M., *Democracy and the Organisation of Political Parties* (London, 1902).

Pahl, R. E., and Winkler, J. T., 'The coming corporation', *New Society*, 10 October 1974.

Parekh, Bhikhu (ed.), *The Concept of Socialism* (Croom Helm, 1975).

Plumb, J. H., *The Death of the Past* (Harmondsworth, 1973).

Pocock, J. G. A., 'Time, institutions and action: an essay on traditions and their understanding', *Politics, Language and Time: Essays on Political Thought and History* (London, 1972), pp. 233–72.

Sorel, G., *Reflections on Violence* (New York, 1962).

Thompson, E. P., *The Making of the English Working Class* (London, 1963).

Thompson, E. P., 'Time, work-discipline and industrial capitalism', *Past and Present*, no. 38, December 1967, pp. 56–97.

Williams, Raymond, *Culture and Society 1780–1950* (Penguin, 1958).

Williams, Raymond, *The Long Revolution* (Penguin, 1971).

Party and organisational theory

Allen, V. L., *Power in Trade Unions: A Study of Their Organization in Great Britain* (London, 1954).

Allen, V. L., *Trade Unions and the Government* (London, 1960).
Beer, S. H., *Modern British Politics: A Study of Parties and Pressure Groups* (London, 1965).
Bray, J., *Decision in Government* (London, 1969).
Butler, D., and Stokes, D., *Political Change in Britain: Forces Shaping Electoral Choice* (Harmondsworth, 1971).
De Jouvenel, B., *Problems of Socialist England* (London, 1949).
Flanders, Allan D., *Trade Unions and the Force of Tradition*, The Sixteenth Fawley Foundation Lecture (Southampton, 1969).
Gamble, Andrew, *The Conservative Nation* (London, 1974).
Gay, P., *The Dilemma of Democratic Socialism: Edward Bernstein's Challenge to Marx* (New York, 1952).
Goldthorpe, J. H., *et al.*, *The Affluent Worker* (Cambridge, 1969).
Hindess, B., *The Decline of Working-Class Politics* (London, 1971).
Houghton (The Rt Hon. Lord Houghton of Sowerby, CH), *Report of the Committee on Financial Aid to Political Parties* (HMSO, 1976).
Jessop, Bob, *Traditionalism, Conservatism and British Political Culture* (London, 1974).
Laski, Harold, *Parliamentary Government in England* (London, 1938).
Lockwood, D., *The Blackcoated Worker* (London, 1958).
McKenzie, R. T., *British Political Parties: The Distribution of Power within the Conservative and Labour Parties*, 2nd edn (London, 1963).
Mackenzie, W. J. M., 'Mr McKenzie on the British parties', *Political Studies*, vol. 3, 1955, pp. 157–9.
Miliband, R., *Parliamentary Socialism: A Study in the Politics of Labour* (London, 1961).
Morrison of Lambeth, Lord, *Government and Parliament: A Survey from the Inside* (London, 1966).
Panitch, Leo, 'Ideology and integration the case of the British Labour Party', *Political Studies*, 1971.
Panitch, Leo, *Social Democracy and Industrial Militancy: The Labour Party, the Trade Unions and Incomes Policy, 1945–1974* (Cambridge, 1976).
Parkin, F., *Class Inequality and Political Order: Social Stratification in Capitalist and Communist Societies* (London, 1972).
Saville, J., 'The Ideology of Labourism', in Benewick, B., Berki, R. N., and Parek, B., *Knowledge and Belief in Politics: The Problems of Ideology* (London, 1974), pp. 213–26.
Rose, R., *The Problem of Party Government* (London, 1974).
Scott, K. J., 'The distribution of power within British parties', *Political Science*, 1956.

The Labour Party General and History:
Abrams, M., and Rose, R., *Must Labour Lose?* (Harmondsworth, 1960).
Anderson, P., 'The origins of the present crisis', *New Left Review*, No. 23, 1964, pp. 26–53.
Attlee, C. R., *As It Happened* (London, 1954).
Attlee, C. R., *The Labour Party in Perspective* (London, 1937).
Bealey, F., and Parkinson, S.,*Unions in Prosperity*, Hobart Paper no. 6 (London, 1960).

128   *Doctrine and Ethos in the Labour Party*

Briggs, A., and Saville, J., *Essays in Labour History in Memory of G. D. H. Cole, 25 September 1889–14 January 1959* (London, 1967).
Briggs, A., and Saville, J., *Essays in Labour History 1886–1923* (London, 1971).
Brown, George, *In My Way: The Political Memoirs of Lord George Brown* (London, 1972).
Bullock, A., *Life and Times Ernest Bevin* (1960).
Cannon, Olga, and Anderson, J. R. L., *The Road from Wigan Pier: A Biography of Les Cannon* (London, 1973).
Coates, David, *The Labour Party and the Struggle for Socialism* (Cambridge, 1975).
Cripps, S., *Problems of a Socialist Government* (London, 1933).
Dalton, H., *Call Back Yesterday* (London, 1953).
Dalton, H., *The Fateful Years: Memoirs 1931–1945* (London, 1957).
Donaughue, Bernard, and Jones, G. W., *Herbert Morrison: Portrait of a Politician* (London, 1973).
Foot, M., *Aneurin Bevan: A Biography, Vol. I, 1897–1945* (London, 1962); *Vol. II, 1945–60* (London, 1973).
Foot, M., *Harold Wilson: A Pictorial Biography* (London, 1964).
Foot, Paul, *The Politics of Harold Wilson* (Harmondsworth, 1968).
Forester, T., *The Labour Party and the Working Class* (London, 1976).
Harrison, M., *Trade Unions and the Labour Party since 1945* (London, 1960).
Haseley, S., *The Gaitskellites: Revisionism in the British Labour Party 1951–64* (London, 1969).
Howell, D., *British Social Democracy* (London, 1976).
Hunter, L., *The Road to Brighton Pier* (London, 1959).
Jenkins, P., *The Battle of Downing Street* (London, 1970).
Jenkins, Roy, *Mr Attlee: An Interim Biography* (London, 1948).
Jenkins, Roy, 'Hugh Gaitskell: a political memoir', *Encounter*, no. 125, February 1964, pp. 3–10.
Keynes, J. M., 'The dilemma of modern socialism', *Political Quarterly*, April 1932, reprinted in Robson, W. A. (ed.), *Political Quarterly in the Thirties* (London, 1971).
Labour Party Reports of the Annual Conference 1901–76.
Layton-Henry, Z., 'Labour's militant youth', *Political Quarterly*, vol. 45, no. 4, October–December 1974, pp. 418–25.
Lee, Jennie, *This Great Journey: A Volume of Autobiography 1904–45* (London, 1963).
Martin, Kingsley, *Harold Laski* (London, 1953).
Middlemas, R. K., *The Clydesiders: A Left Wing Struggle for Parliamentary Power* (London, 1965).
Miliband, R., 'Socialism and the myth of the golden past', in Miliband, R., and Saville, J. (eds), *The Socialist Register 1964*, pp. 92–104.
Nairn, T., 'The nature of the Labour Party I', *New Left Review*, no. 27, 1964, pp. 38–65.
Nairn, T., 'The nature of the Labour Party II', *New Left Review*, no. 28, 1964, pp. 33–63.
Pelling, H., *A Short History of the Labour Party* (London 1965).

Roberts, R., *The Classic Slum Life in Scotland in the First Quarter of This Century* (Harmondsworth 1973).
Seyd, P., 'The Tavernite', *Political Quarterly*, vol. 45, no. 2, April–June 1974, pp. 243–5.
Skidelsky, R., '1929–31 revisited', *Society for the Study of Labour History, Bulletin no. 20*, 1970.
Wertheimer, Egan, *Portrait of the Labour Party* (London, 1929).
Williams, Marcia, *Inside No. 10* (London, 1975).
Wilson, Harold, *The Labour Government 1964–70: A Personal Record* (London, 1971).

Policies:
Beveridge, W. H., *Full Employment in a Free Society* (London, 1944).
Beveridge, W. H., *Planning Under Socialism and Other Addresses* (London, 1936).
Boyle, E., Crosland, A., and Kogan, M., *The Politics of Education* (Harmondsworth, 1971).
Brittan, S., *Steering the Economy: The Role of the Treasury* (Harmondsworth, 1971).
Brown, Gordon, *The Red Paper for Scotland* (Edinburgh, 1975).
Chester, N., *The Nationalization of British Industry 1945–51* (London, 1975).
Crossman, R. H. S., *Inside View* (Cape, 1972).
Crossman, R. H. S., *The Diaries of a Cabinet Minister*, Vol. I, *Minister of Housing* (London, 1976).
Davis, W., *Three Years Hard Labour: The Road to Devaluation* (London, 1968).
Dennis, N., *People and Planning: The Sociology of Housing in Sunderland* (London, 1972).
Dennis, N., *et al.*, *Coal Is Our Life* (London, 1956).
Dorfman, Gerald A., *Wage Politics in Britain, 1945–1967* (Ames, Iowa, 1973).
Epstein, L., 'Who makes British party policy? British Labour, 1960–61', *Midwest Journal of Political Science*, vol. VI, no. 2, May 1962, pp. 165–72.
Gaitskell, H., 'Public ownership and equality', *Socialist Commentary*, vol. XIX, June 1955, pp. 165–7.
Gellner, Ernest, 'A social contract in search of an idiom', *Political Quarterly*, vol. 46, no. 2, April–June 1975, pp. 127–52.
Hanson, A. H., 'Labour and the Public Corporation', *Public Administration*, Summer 1954, pp. 203–9.
Hunt, Norman, *Whitehall and Beyond* [Conversations with Jo Grimond, Enoch Powell and Harold Wilson] London, 1964).
Jenkins, Roy, 'In and out of power', *Observer*, 20 June 1971.
Jenkins, Roy, 'The reality of political power', *Sunday Times*, 17 January 1971.
Kelf-Cohen, R., *Nationalisation in Britain: The End of a Dogma* (London, 1961).
Mitchell, Austin, 'Clay Cross', *Political Quarterly*, vol. 45, no. 2, April–June 1974, pp. 165–78.

Oldfield, A., 'The Labour Party and planning – 1934 and 1918?' *Society for the Study of Labour History, Bulletin no. 25*, Autumn 1962, pp. 41–55.

Ostergaard, Geoffrey, 'Labour and the development of the public corporation', *Manchester School of Economic and Social Studies*, May 1954, pp. 192–226.

Saville, J., 'Labour and income distribution', in Miliband, R., and Saville, J., *The Socialist Register 1965*, pp. 147–62.

Share, P., *Entitled to Know* (London, 1966).

Sharpe, L. J., 'How the Labour Party evolves policies', *New Society*, vol. 21, no. 511, 1973, pp. 66–9.

Tawney, R. H., *The Radical Tradition* (Harmondsworth, 1966).

Taylor, Robert, 'The uneasy alliance – Labour and the unions', *Political Quarterly*, vol. 47, no. 4, October–December 1976, pp. 398–407.

Titmus, R. M., *Income Distribution and Social Change: A Study in Criticism* (London, 1962).

Townsend, P., and Bosanquet, N., *Labour and Inequality* (London, 1972).

Vann, Neil, 'A better way to Labour's programme', *Socialist Commentary*, October 1976, pp. 10–11.

Wedderburn, Dorothy (ed.), *Poverty, Inequality and Class Structure* (London, 1974).

Wilson, J. H., 'Where the power lies', *The Listener*, 9 February 1967, pp. 183–5.

Wootton, B., *Plan or No Plan* (London, 1934).

Young, M., *Is Equality a Dream?* (First Rita Hinden Memorial Lecture), November 1972.

Labour ideology

Alexander, K. J. W., and Hobbs, A., 'What influences Labour MPs?' *New Society*, 13 December 1962, pp. 11–14.

Barker, R., *Education and Politics 1900–1951: A Study of the Labour Party* (Oxford, 1972).

Barratt-Brown, M., *From Labourism to Socialism* (London, 1972).

Barry, E. Eldon, *Nationalisation in British Politics* (London, 1965).

Benn, Anthony Wedgewood, *The Regeneration of Britain* (London, 1964).

Bevan, Aneurin, *In Place of Fear* (London, 1952).

Bevan, Aneurin, *Why Not Trust the Tories* (London, 1944).

Coates, Ken, *The Crisis of British Socialism: Essays on the Rise of Harold Wilson and the Fall of the Labour Party* (Nottingham, 1972).

Crosland, C. A. R., *Future of Socialism* (London, 1956).

Crosland, C. A. R., *Social Democracy in Europe*, Fabian Tract 438, December 1975.

Crosland, C. A. R., *Socialism, Land and Equality* (*Second Rita Hinden Memorial Lecture*), 1973.

Crosland, C. A. R., *Socialism Now and Other Essays* (London, 1974).

Crossman, R. H. S. (ed.), *New Fabian Essays* (London, 1970).

Crossman, R. H. S., 'Socialism and planning', in Rodgers, W. (ed.), *Socialism and Affluence: Four Fabian Essays*, May 1967, pp. 70–93.

Crossman, R. H. S., *Planning for Freedom* (London, 1965).
Durbin, E., *The Politics of Democratic Socialism* (London, 1940).
Gaitskell, H., 'Socialism and nationalisation', Fabian Tract 300, July 1956.
Harrison, Royden, 'Labour government: then and now', *Political Quarterly*, vol. 41, no. 1, January–March 1970, pp. 67–82.
Holland, Stuart, *The Socialist Challenge* (London, 1975).
Jay, Douglas, *The Socialist Case* (London, n.d. [1937?]).
Jenkins, Peter, 'The social democratic dilemma', *The New Statesman*, 20 September 1974, pp. 373–8.
Jenkins, Roy, 'Equality', in Crossman, R. H. S. (ed.), *New Fabian Essays* (London, 1952), pp. 69–90.
Jenkins, Roy, *What Matters Now* (Redhill, 1972).
Mackintosh, J. P., 'Socialism or social democracy? The choice for the Labour Party', *Political Quarterly*, vol. 43, no. 4, 1972, pp. 470–84.
Tawney, R. H., *The Acquisitive Society* (London, 1961).
Tawney, R. H., *Equality* (London, 1931).
Vaizey, John, *et al.*, 'Whatever happened to equality? Six discussions', *The Listener*, 2, 9, 16, 23, 30 May, 6 June 1974.
Williams, R. (ed.), *May Day Manifesto 1968* (Harmondsworth, 1968).

Index

134   Doctrine and Ethos in the Labour Party

Parties: Communist 30, 31, 106, 107; Conservatives 1, 4, 5, 11, 13, 17, 19, 24–5, 37, 38, 41, 45, 56, 57, 63, 64, 93, 94, 100, 103, 107, 108, 113, 117–18; Labour, *see* Labour Party; Liberals 9, 11, 19, 25, 56, 57, 75, 93, 113, 120; National Front 109, 120; Scottish and Welsh Nationalist 120; Scottish Labour Party 119; Social Democratic (Germany) 89, 98; Third Parties and Coalitions 106–7, 117–20

Pelling, H. and Hinton, J. 10, 20, 125

Police Service 4, 80

Policies 11, 82, 92, 98; as 'projects' 25, 41; child benefit 62; defence and disarmament 9, 28, 96, 108; education 9, 11, 19, 49, 56, 57, 59, 74, 98–9; foreign *see* Foreign Policy; housing 4, 82–3, 114; job creation scheme 62; national health scheme 9, 36, 37, 38, 54, 57, 74, 79–80, 86, 96, 107; pensions 82; taxation 9, 37, 54, 62, 82, 114; unemployment 4, 63–65, 71, 81, 108–9; wage and price controls 81; welfare state 54–7, 74

Poor Law 20, 36

Poverty and Inequality 57–8, 62

Prentice, R. 94, 102

Public Sector 46–7, 74, 77

Robens, A. 14

Roberts, R. 20, 21

Robertson, J. 119

Rose, R. 15, 47, 114

Rowntree, B. S. and Lavers, G. R. 54–6

Schon, D. 18

Scotland 34, 72, 78, 80, 82

Second World War 41, 63, 85, 86

Sharpe, Dame E. 102

Shaw, B. 8

Shawcross, H. 14, 99

Sillars, J. 119

Skeffington report 85

Skidelsky, R. 4, 75

Smiles, S. 15

Smith, A. 7

Snowden 13, 36, 122, 123

SDF (Social Democratic Federation) 30

Socialism 12, 25–6, 41; achievement of 25–6, 41, 71, 91, 95, 107; as class struggle 3, 7–8, 31, 39, 53; as consolidationism 43; as corporate socialism 8, 45, 87, 116; as egalitarianism 5, 9, 44–65, 107–10; as nationalisation 28, 38, 43, 46–9; as planning 26–7, 68–87, 107, 110; as revisionism/social democracy 28–9, 44–9, 52–9, 89–91, 97, 100, 104; Parliamentary socialism 4, 69–70, 98, 115

Steel, D. 119

Steel nationalisation 79, 107, 114

Strachey, J. 29, 70

Swift, J. 96

Swing Captain 26

Taff Vale 18, 36

Taverne, R. 14, 119

Tawney, R. 8, 27, 28, 49, 50, 51, 52, 53

Thatcher, M. 117

Thompson, E. P. 7

Titmuss, R. M. 56, 57, 58

Tolpuddle Martyrs 32

Townsend, P. and Bosanquet 57

Trade Unions 3, 6, 11, 12, 15, 17, 18, 25, 30, 37, 38, 39, 40, 45, 50, 59–63, 64–5, 78, 81, 94, 109, 114, 116–17, 120

Tribune Group 11, 43, 92

Walker, M. 109

Webb, S. and B. 8, 27, 71, 72, 83, 123

Wheatly, J. 30

Williams, F. 73

Williams, R. 26

Wilson, H. 1, 6, 14, 26, 76, 101, 103, 124

Winter, J. M. 27

Wise, E. F. 71

Wooton, B. 72, 73

Working Classes 3, 5, 7, 9, 11, 18, 21, 25, 33, 36, 40–1, 50

Wright Mills, C. 91